D1067698

THE ENGLISH ASSOCIATION

(Founded 1906)

President (1920-21)

The Right Hon. Archbishop of York, P.C., D.D.

Chairman of Committee: Miss M. E. Adams, M.A., Newnham College, Cambridge

The object of the English Association is to promote the knowledge and appreciation of the English language and of English literature, and to uphold the standards of English writing and speech.

It seeks to attain these objects by spreading the opportunities for intercourse and co-operation amongst all those interested in English language and literature; by furthering the due recognition of English in our national scheme of education; by discussing the methods of teaching English and by watching and, if need be, taking action in English language and literary questions, especially; and endeavouring to discover the defects of the literature by publishing periodical books, papers, and leaflets to promote the study of literature; by furnishing expert lectures to carry out the object of the Association, and by establishing, working with kindred bodies and co-operating with such societies; by furtherance of the object of the Association; by affording facilities for bringing students from institutions and universities into connection, to the object of the Association; and by means of any other activity which shall be conducive to the object of the Association.

Membership

The Association will now form branches in connection with the central Association.

The Annual Subscription to the Association is 10s. 6d., paid to the Honorary Treasurer.

Communications should be addressed to the Honorary Secretary.

Subscriptions should be sent to the Honorary Treasurer.

THE ENGLISH ASSOCIATION

8 CROMWELL PLACE, LONDON, S.W.7

Secretary: A. V. HOUGHTON

Publishers: H. M. FILLANS

Oxford: Humphrey Milford
London: SIMPKIN, MARSHALL, & CO.

THE ENGLISH ASSOCIATION

(FOUNDED 1906)

President 1959/60 :

HIS GRACE THE ARCHBISHOP OF YORK, P.C., D.D.

Chairman of Committee: Instr. Rear-Admiral SIR ARTHUR HALL, K.B.E., C.B.

The object of the English Association is to promote the knowledge and appreciation of the English language and of English literature, and to uphold the standards of English writing and speech.

The Association pursues this object by affording opportunities for intercourse and co-operation amongst all those interested in English language and literature, by furthering the due recognition of English as an essential element in education; by discussing methods of teaching English and by encouraging and facilitating advanced study in English language and literature; by holding conferences, lectures and other meetings to further the object of the Association; by publishing a journal, books, papers and leaflets to promote the study of English; by forming local branches to carry out the object of the Association; and by establishing relations with kindred bodies and co-operating with such bodies in furtherance of the object of the Association; by enrolling members and collecting subscriptions from members and donations from any person interested in the object of the Association; and by engaging in any other activity which shall be conducive to the object of the Association.

SUBSCRIPTIONS

The financial year runs from 1st January to 31st December, and an ordinary subscription paid at any time during the year entitles a member to the Association's magazine ENGLISH (three issues) and the Presidential Address.

The annual subscription to the Central Body is £1 1s., or, with *Essays and Studies* (New Series) and *The Year's Work in English Studies*, £2 2s., and is due on the 1st January.

Life Membership (which does not cover the two special publications *Essays and Studies* and *The Year's Work in English Studies*) is £15 15s.

The annual subscription of branch members is fixed within certain limits by the branch.

CORPORATE membership (£1 1s. or £2 2s.) is open to Colleges, Schools and Libraries and additional publications can be purchased at the reduced rate.

STUDENT membership is open on special terms to students up to the age of 23 who are interested in English Language and Literature.

Subscriptions should be sent to the Secretary, 8 Cromwell Place, London, S.W.7. (Cheques, etc., should be made in favour of the English Association.)

The Headquarters of the Association are
8 CROMWELL PLACE, LONDON, S.W.7
(Telephone : KENSINGTON 8480)

Organising Officer: MR. E. WYNNE HICKIE

Secretary: MRS. E. M. FIELDING

Auditors: Messrs. P. D. LEAKE & Co., 84 Queen Victoria Street, E.C.4.

Bankers: BARCLAYS BANK, Ltd., 95 Victoria Street, Westminster, S.W.1.

Poems of To-Day

Poems of To-Day:

an Anthology

DISCARDED

London:
Published for the English Association
by Sidgwick & Jackson, Ltd.

First issued in August, 1915 ;
Reprinted October, 1915 ; *January, March,
June, September, and December,* 1916;
May, July, September, October, 1917 ;
January, February, July, and November, 1918 ;
May and October, 1919 ;
May and September, 1920 ;
January, March, and September, 1921 ;
January, June, and July, 1922 ;
January, March, and October, 1923 ;
February and October, 1924 ;
June and October, 1925 ;
September, October, and December, 1926 ;
July, 1928 ; *April, June,* 1929 ;
Reprinted October, 1929 ; *January and August,* 1930;
January and February, 1931 ;
July and October, 1932 ;
September and October, 1934 ;
February and October, 1935 ;
October and December, 1936 ;
September, 1937 ; *September,* 1938 ;
January and June, 1941 ;
May and August, 1942 ;
October, 1943; *April,* 1944;
October, 1945; *March,* 1946;
August, 1946; *September,* 1947;
January and September, 1948;
December, 1949; *December,* 1952;
December, 1955; *June,* 1960

PRINTED AND BOUND IN ENGLAND BY
HAZELL WATSON AND VINEY LTD
AYLESBURY AND SLOUGH

PR
1224
.P6

KR

Colonial 1967

PREFATORY NOTE

THIS book has been compiled in order that boys and girls, already perhaps familiar with the great classics of the English speech, may also know something of the newer poetry of their own day. Most of the writers are living, and the rest are still vivid memories among us, while one of the youngest, almost as these words are written, has gone singing to lay down his life for his country's cause. Although no definite chronological limit has been set, and Meredith at least began to write in the middle of the nineteenth century, the intention has been to represent mainly those poetic tendencies which have become dominant as the influence of the accepted Victorian masters has grown weaker, and from which the poetry of the future, however it may develop, must in turn take its start. It may be helpful briefly to indicate the sequence of themes. Man draws his being from the heroic Past and from the Earth his Mother ; and in harmony with these he must shape his life to what high purposes he may. Therefore this gathering of poems falls into three groups.

110278

First there are poems of History, of the romantic tale of the world, of our own special tradition here in England, and of the inheritance of obligation which that tradition imposes upon us. Naturally, there are some poems directly inspired by the present war, but nothing, it is hoped, which may not, in happier days, bear translation into any European tongue. Then there come poems of the Earth, of England again and the longing of the exile for home, of this and that familiar countryside, of woodland and meadow and garden, of the process of the seasons, of the " open road " and the " wind on the heath," of the city, its deprivations and its consolations. Finally there are poems of Life itself, of the moods in which it may be faced, of religion, of man's excellent virtues, of friendship and childhood, of passion, grief, and comfort. But there is no arbitrary isolation of one theme from another; they mingle and inter-penetrate throughout, to the music of Pan's flute, and of Love's viol, and the bugle-call of Endeavour, and the passing-bell of Death.

May, 1915.

INDEX OF AUTHORS

For permission to use copyright poems the English Association is greatly indebted to the authors ; to the literary executors of Mary Coleridge (Sir Henry Newbolt), J. E. Flecker (Mrs. Flecker), Lionel Johnson (Mr. Elkin Mathews), George Meredith (Trustees, through Mr. W. M. Meredith), R. L. Stevenson (Mr. Lloyd Osbourne), Arthur Symons (through Mr. Edmund Gosse), and Francis Thompson (Mr. Wilfrid Meynell) ; and to the following publishers in respect of the poems enumerated :

Mr. B. H. Blackwell :
A. S. Cripps, *Lyra Evangelistica* (Nos. 25, 26, 39).

Messrs. W. Blackwood & Sons :
Alfred Noyes, *Drake* (No. 12).

Mr. A. H. Bullen :
W. B. Yeats, *Poems* (Nos. 101, 133, 146).

Messrs. Burns & Oates :
Francis Thompson, *Works* (Nos. 105, 106, 110, 123, 127, 145).
Alice Meynell, *Collected Poems* (Nos. 62, 74, 81, 107, 111, 115, 137, 140, 147).
Shane Leslie, *Eyes of Youth* (No. 84).

Messrs. Chatto & Windus :
R. L. Stevenson, *Underwoods* (Nos. 51, 73, 90, 109), and
Songs of Travel (Nos. 29, 32, 68, 71, 94, 96, 135).

Messrs. Constable & Co. :
Walter de la Mare, *The Listeners* (Nos 1, 61, 67, 117, 142).

Messrs. J. M. Dent & Sons, Ltd. :
  W. Canton, *The Comrades* (No. 28).
  G. K. Chesterton, *The Wild Knight* (No. 131).

Messrs. Duckworth & Co. :
  Hilaire Belloc, *Verses* (Nos. 35, 45, 112).
  T. Sturge Moore, *The Gazelles* (Nos. 89, 93).

Mr. A. C. Fifield :
  W. H. Davies, *Songs of Joy* (Nos. 48, 86), and
                Nature Poems (No. 53).

Messrs. Max Goschen, Ltd. :
  J. E. Flecker, *The Golden Journey to Samarcand* * (Nos. 24, 60).

Mr. William Heinemann :
  W. S. Blunt, *Poetry of* (Nos. 36, 64, 65).
  Edmund Gosse, *Collected Poems* (Nos. 82, 87).
  Arthur Symons, *Poems* (Nos. 85, 113, 130).

Mr. John Lane :
  L. Abercrombie, *Interludes and Poems* (No. 31).
  John Davidson, *Ballads and Songs* (Nos. 37, 38, 80).
  William Watson, *The Hope of the World* (Nos. 66, 121).
  Margaret L. Woods, *Lyrics and Ballads* (Nos. 10, 91).

Mr. Elkin Mathews :
  Laurence Binyon, *Poems* (1894), (No. 79),
                   London Visions (Nos. 75, 77), and
                   England (Nos. 16, 57, 129).
  Lionel Johnson, *Poems* (Nos. 9, 95, 118).

Messrs. Maunsel & Co. :
  P. R. Chalmers, *Green Days and Blue Days* (No. 99).
  Padraic Colum, *Wild Earth* (No. 124).

Messrs. Methuen & Co. :
  Rudyard Kipling, *The Seven Seas* (No. 50), and
                   The Five Nations (No. 34).
  Sir A. T. Quiller-Couch, *Poems and Ballads* (No. 8), and
                           The Vigil of Venus (No. 44).
  Herbert Trench, *New Poems* (Nos. 14, 92).

         * Now transferred to Mr. Martin Secker.

Messrs. Sidgwick & Jackson, Ltd. :
 Rupert Brooke, *1914 and Other Poems* (Nos. 20, 21, 47).
 John Drinkwater, *Swords and Ploughshares* (Nos. 19, 40, 41).
 Laurence Housman, *Selected Poems* (No. 83).
 Rose Macaulay, *The Two Blind Countries* (No. 46).

Messrs. Smith, Elder & Co. :
 Robert Bridges, *Poetical Works* (Nos. 54, 56, 63, 76, 104, 125, 126, 128, 132, 139, 141).

Messrs. T. Fisher Unwin, Ltd. :
 Ernest Radford, *Poems* (No. 42).
 W. B. Yeats, *Poems* (Nos. 49, 88, 138, 143, 144).

The Poetry Book Shop (through Mr. Harold Monro).
 Ralph Hodgson, *Eve* (No. 5).

The Editor of *The Times* courteously confirmed the permissions given by Mr. George Russell (" A. E.") in respect of No. 23, and by Mr. Laurence Binyon in respect of No. 22—the latter being reprinted in *The Winnowing Fan* (Elkin Mathews).

The Association desires also to acknowledge the generosity with which authors and publishers have waived or reduced customary copyright fees, in view of the special objects of their organisation. They regret that considerations of copyright have rendered it impossible to include poems by T. E. Brown, Thomas Hardy, W. E. Henley, and A. E. Housman.

POEMS OF TO-DAY

1. ALL THAT'S PAST

VERY old are the woods;
    And the buds that break
Out of the briar's boughs,
    When March winds wake,
So old with their beauty are—
    Oh, no man knows
Through what wild centuries
    Roves back the rose.

Very old are the brooks;
    And the rills that rise
Where snow sleeps cold beneath
    The azure skies
Sing such a history
    Of come and gone,
Their every drop is as wise
    As Solomon.

Very old are we men;
    Our dreams are tales
Told in dim Eden
    By Eve's nightingales;

We wake and whisper awhile,
  But, the day gone by,
Silence and sleep like fields
  Of amaranth lie.

Walter de la Mare.

2. PRE-EXISTENCE

I LAID me down upon the shore
  And dreamed a little space ;
I heard the great waves break and roar ;
  The sun was on my face.

My idle hands and fingers brown
  Played with the pebbles grey ;
The waves came up, the waves went down,
  Most thundering and gay.

The pebbles, they were smooth and round
  And warm upon my hands,
Like little people I had found
  Sitting among the sands.

The grains of sands so shining-small
  Soft through my fingers ran ;
The sun shone down upon it all,
  And so my dream began :

How all of this had been before ;
  How ages far away
I lay on some forgotten shore
  As here I lie to-day.

The waves came shining up the sands,
　As here to-day they shine ;
And in my pre-pelasgian hands
　The sand was warm and fine.

I have forgotten whence I came,
　Or what my home might be,
Or by what strange and savage name
　I called that thundering sea.

I only know the sun shone down
　As still it shines to-day,
And in my fingers long and brown
　The little pebbles lay.

Frances Cornford.

3. FRAGMENTS

Troy Town is covered up with weeds,
　The rabbits and the pismires brood
On broken gold, and shards, and beads
　Where Priam's ancient palace stood.

The floors of many a gallant house
　Are matted with the roots of grass ;
The glow-worm and the nimble mouse
　Among her ruins flit and pass.

And there, in orts of blackened bone,
　The widowed Trojan beauties lie,
And Simois babbles over stone
　And waps and gurgles to the sky.

Once there were merry days in Troy,
  Her chimneys smoked with cooking meals,
The passing chariots did annoy
  The sunning housewives at their wheels.

And many a lovely Trojan maid
  Set Trojan lads to lovely things ;
The game of life was nobly played,
  They played the game like Queens and Kings.

So that, when Troy had greatly passed
  In one red roaring fiery coal,
The courts the Grecians overcast
  Became a city in the soul.

In some green island of the sea,
  Where now the shadowy coral grows
In pride and pomp and empery
  The courts of old Atlantis rose.

In many a glittering house of glass
  The Atlanteans wandered there ;
The paleness of their faces was
  Like ivory, so pale they were.

And hushed they were, no noise of words
  In those bright cities ever rang ;
Only their thoughts, like golden birds,
  About their chambers thrilled and sang.

They knew all wisdom, for they knew
  The souls of those Egyptian Kings

Who learned, in ancient Babilu,
  The beauty of immortal things.

They knew all beauty—when they thought
  The air chimed like a stricken lyre,
The elemental birds were wrought,
  The golden birds became a fire.

And straight to busy camps and marts
  The singing flames were swiftly gone ;
The trembling leaves of human hearts
  Hid boughs for them to perch upon.

And men in desert places, men
  Abandoned, broken, sick with fears,
Rose singing, swung their swords agen,
  And laughed and died among the spears.

The green and greedy seas have drowned
  That city's glittering walls and towers,
Her sunken minarets are crowned
  With red and russet water-flowers.

In towers and rooms and golden courts
  The shadowy coral lifts her sprays ;
The scrawl hath gorged her broken orts,
  The shark doth haunt her hidden ways.

But, at the falling of the tide,
  The golden birds still sing and gleam,
The Atlanteans have not died,
  Immortal things still give us dream.

The dream that fires man's heart to make,
    To build, to do, to sing or say
A beauty Death can never take,
    An Adam from the crumbled clay.
                                        John Masefield.

4. FALLEN CITIES

I GATHERED with a careless hand
    There where the waters night and day
    Are languid in the idle bay,
A little heap of golden sand ;
    And, as I saw it, in my sight
    Awoke a vision brief and bright,
A city in a pleasant land.

I saw no mound of earth, but fair
    Turrets and domes and citadels,
    With murmuring of many bells ;
The spires were white in the blue air,
    And men by thousands went and came,
    Rapid and restless, and like flame
Blown by their passions here and there.

With careless hand I swept away
    The little mound before I knew ;
    The visioned city vanished too,
And fall'n beneath my fingers lay.
    Ah God ! how many hast Thou seen
    Cities that are not and have been,
By silent hill and idle bay !
                                        Gerald Gould.

5. TIME, YOU OLD GIPSY MAN

Time, you old gipsy man,
　　Will you not stay,
Put up your caravan
　　Just for one day?

All things I'll give you,
Will you be my guest,
Bells for your jennet
Of silver the best,
Goldsmiths shall beat you
A great golden ring,
Peacocks shall bow to you,
Little boys sing,
Oh, and sweet girls will
Festoon you with may,
Time, you old gipsy,
Why hasten away?

Last week in Babylon,
Last night in Rome,
Morning, and in the crush
Under Paul's dome;
Under Paul's dial
You tighten your rein—
Only a moment,
And off once again;
Off to some city
Now blind in the womb,
Off to another
Ere that's in the tomb.

Time, you old gipsy man,
　　Will you not stay,
Put up your caravan
　　Just for one day ?

Ralph Hodgson.

6. A HUGUENOT

O, A gallant set were they,
　　As they charged on us that day,
A thousand riding like one !
　　Their trumpets crying,
　　And their white plumes flying,
And their sabres flashing in the sun.

O, a sorry lot were we,
　　As we stood beside the sea,
Each man for himself as he stood !
　　We were scattered and lonely—
　　A little force only
Of the good men fighting for the good.

But I never loved more
　　On sea or on shore
The ringing of my own true blade,
　　Like lightning it quivered,
　　And the hard helms shivered,
As I sang, " None maketh me afraid ! "

Mary E. Coleridge.

7. ON THE TOILET TABLE OF QUEEN MARIE-ANTOINETTE

THIS was her table, these her trim outspread
 Brushes and trays and porcelain cups for red ;
Here sate she, while her women tired and curled
The most unhappy head in all the world.

       J. B. B. Nichols.

8. UPON ECKINGTON BRIDGE, RIVER AVON

O PASTORAL heart of England ! like a psalm
 Of green days telling with a quiet beat—
O wave into the sunset flowing calm !
 O tirèd lark descending on the wheat !
Lies it all peace beyond that western fold
 Where now the lingering shepherd sees his star
Rise upon Malvern ?   Paints an Age of Gold
 Yon cloud with prophecies of linkèd ease—
 Lulling this Land, with hills drawn up like knees,
To drowse beside her implements of war ?

Man shall outlast his battles.   They have swept
 Avon from Naseby Field to Severn Ham ;
And Evesham's dedicated stones have stepp'd
 Down to the dust with Montfort's oriflamme.
Nor the red tear nor the reflected tower
 Abides ; but yet these eloquent grooves remain,
Worn in the sandstone parapet hour by hour
 By labouring bargemen where they shifted ropes.
 E'en so shall man turn back from violent hopes
To Adam's cheer, and toil with spade again.

  P.T.D. I—I*

Ay, and his mother Nature, to whose lap
  Like a repentant child at length he hies,
Not in the whirlwind or the thunder-clap
  Proclaims her more tremendous mysteries :
But when in winter's grave, bereft of light,
  With still, small voice divinelier whispering
—Lifting the green head of the aconite,
  Feeding with sap of hope the hazel-shoot—
  She feels God's finger active at the root,
Turns in her sleep, and murmurs of the Spring.
                              Arthur Quiller-Couch.

9. BY THE STATUE OF KING CHARLES AT CHARING CROSS

SOMBRE and rich, the skies ;
    Great glooms, and starry plains.
Gently the night wind sighs ;
Else a vast silence reigns.

The splendid silence clings
Around me : and around
The saddest of all kings
Crowned, and again discrowned.

Comely and calm, he rides
Hard by his own Whitehall :
Only the night wind glides :
No crowds, nor rebels, brawl.

Gone, too, his Court : and yet,
The stars his courtiers are :
Stars in their stations set ;
And every wandering star.

Alone he rides, alone,
The fair and fatal king :
Dark night is all his own,
That strange and solemn thing.

Which are more full of fate :
The stars ; or those sad eyes ?
Which are more still and great :
Those brows ; or the dark skies ?

Although his whole heart yearn
In passionate tragedy :
Never was face so stern
With sweet austerity.

Vanquished in life, his death
By beauty made amends :
The passing of his breath
Won his defeated ends.

Brief life and hapless ?   Nay :
Through death, life grew sublime.
Speak after sentence ?   Yea :
And to the end of time.

Armoured he rides, his head
Bare to the stars of doom :
He triumphs now, the dead,
Beholding London's gloom.

Our wearier spirit faints,
Vexed in the world's employ :

His soul was of the saints ;
And art to him was joy.

King, tried in fires of woe !
Men hunger for thy grace :
And through the night I go,
Loving thy mournful face.

Yet when the city sleeps ;
When all the cries are still :
The stars and heavenly deeps
Work out a perfect will.

Lionel Johnson.

10. TO THE FORGOTTEN DEAD

To the forgotten dead,
    Come, let us drink in silence ere we part.
To every fervent yet resolvèd heart
That brought its tameless passion and its tears,
Renunciation and laborious years,
To lay the deep foundations of our race,
To rear its stately fabric overhead
And light its pinnacles with golden grace.
    To the unhonoured dead.

To the forgotten dead,
Whose dauntless hands were stretched to grasp the
    rein
Of Fate and hurl into the void again
Her thunder-hoofèd horses, rushing blind
Earthward along the courses of the wind.

Among the stars, along the wind in vain
Their souls were scattered and their blood was shed,
And nothing, nothing of them doth remain.
    To the thrice-perished dead.
                Margaret L. Woods.

11. DRAKE'S DRUM

DRAKE he's in his hammock an' a thousand mile
    away,
  (Capten, art tha sleepin' there below ?)
Slung atween the round shot in Nombre Dios Bay,
  An' dreamin' arl the time o' Plymouth Hoe.
Yarnder lumes the Island, yarnder lie the ships,
  Wi' sailor-lads a-dancin' heel-an'-toe,
An' the shore-lights flashin', an' the night-tide dashin',
  He sees et arl so plainly as he saw et long ago.

Drake he was a Devon man, an' ruled the Devon seas,
  (Capten, art tha sleepin' there below ?)
Rovin' tho' his death fell, he went wi' heart at ease,
  An' dreamin' arl the time o' Plymouth Hoe.
" Take my drum to England, hang et by the shore,
  Strike et when your powder's runnin' low ;
If the Dons sight Devon, I'll quit the port o' Heaven,
  An' drum them up the Channel as we drummed
    them long ago."

Drake he's in his hammock till the great Armadas
  come,
  (Capten, art tha sleepin' there below ?)
Slung atween the round shot, listenin' for the drum,
  An' dreamin' arl the time o' Plymouth Hoe.

Call him on the deep sea, call him up the Sound,
  Call him when ye sail to meet the foe ;
Where the old trade's plyin' an' the old flag flyin'
  They shall find him ware an' wakin', as they found
    him long ago !

                              Henry Newbolt.

12. THE MOON IS UP

THE moon is up : the stars are bright :
    The wind is fresh and free !
We're out to seek for gold to-night
    Across the silver sea !
The world was growing grey and old :
    Break out the sails again !
We're out to seek a Realm of Gold
    Beyond the Spanish Main.

We're sick of all the cringing knees,
    The courtly smiles and lies !
God, let Thy singing Channel breeze
    Lighten our hearts and eyes !
Let love no more be bought and sold
    For earthly loss or gain ;
We're out to seek an Age of Gold
    Beyond the Spanish Main.

Beyond the light of far Cathay,
    Beyond all mortal dreams,
Beyond the reach of night and day
    Our El Dorado gleams,

Revealing—as the skies unfold—
 A star without a stain,
The Glory of the Gates of Gold
 Beyond the Spanish Main.
                              Alfred Noyes.

13. MINORA SIDERA

SITTING at times over a hearth that burns
 With dull domestic glow,
My thought, leaving the book, gratefully turns
 To you who planned it so.

Not of the great only you deigned to tell—
 The stars by which we steer—
But lights out of the night that flashed, and fell
 To night again, are here.

Such as were those, dogs of an elder day,
 Who sacked the golden ports,
And those later who dared grapple their prey
 Beneath the harbour forts :

Some with flag at the fore, sweeping the world
 To find an equal fight,
And some who joined war to their trade, and hurled
 Ships of the line in flight.

Whether their fame centuries long should ring
 They cared not over-much,
But cared greatly to serve God and the king,
 And keep the Nelson touch ;

And fought to build Britain above the tide
  Of wars and windy fate ;
And passed content, leaving to us the pride
  Of lives obscurely great.

Henry Newbolt.

14. MUSING ON A GREAT SOLDIER

*F*EAR? *Yes . . .* I heard you saying
    In an Oxford common-room
Where the hearth-light's kindly raying
Stript the empanelled walls of gloom,
Silver groves of candles playing
In the soft wine turned to bloom—
At the word I see you now
Blandly push the wine-boat's prow
Round the mirror of that scored
Yellow old mahogany board—
I confess to one fear ; this,
To be buried alive !

My Lord,
Your fancy has played amiss.

Fear not.   When in farewell
While guns toll like a bell
And the bell tolls like a gun
Westminster towers call
Folk and state to your funeral,
And robed in honours won,
Beneath the cloudy pall
Of the lifted shreds of glory

You lie in the last stall
Of that grey dormitory—
Fear not lest mad mischance
Should find you lapt and shrouded
Alive in helpless trance
Though seeming death-beclouded :

For long ere so you rest
On that transcendent bier
Shall we not have addressed
One summons, one last test,
To your reluctant ear ?
O believe it ! we shall have uttered
In ultimate entreaty
A name your soul would hear
Howsoever thickly shuttered ;
We shall have stooped and muttered
England ! in your cold ear. . .
Then, if your great pulse leap
No more, nor your cheek burn,
Enough ; then shall we learn
'Tis time for us to weep.

Herbert Trench.

15. HE FELL AMONG THIEVES

" YE have robbed," said he, " ye have slaughtered
        and made an end,
Take your ill-got plunder, and bury the dead :
What will ye more of your guest and sometime
    friend ? "
" Blood for our blood," they said.

He laughed : " If one may settle the score for five,
   I am ready ; but let the reckoning stand till day :
I have loved the sunlight as dearly as any alive."
   " You shall die at dawn," said they.

He flung his empty revolver down the slope,
   He climb'd alone to the Eastward edge of the trees ;
All night long in a dream untroubled of hope
   He brooded, clasping his knees.

He did not hear the monotonous roar that fills
   The ravine where the Yassin river sullenly flows ;
He did not see the starlight on the Laspur hills,
   Or the far Afghan snows.

He saw the April noon on his books aglow,
   The wistaria trailing in at the window wide ;
He heard his father's voice from the terrace below
   Calling him down to ride.

He saw the gray little church across the park,
   The mounds that hid the loved and honoured dead ;
The Norman arch, the chancel softly dark,
   The brasses black and red.

He saw the School Close, sunny and green,
   The runner beside him, the stand by the parapet
     wall,
The distant tape, and the crowd roaring between
   His own name over all.

He saw the dark wainscot and timbered roof,
   The long tables, and the faces merry and keen ;
The College Eight and their trainer dining aloof,
   The Dons on the daïs serene.

He watch'd the liner's stem ploughing the foam,
   He felt her trembling speed and the thrash of her
      screw ;
He heard her passengers' voices talking of home,
   He saw the flag she flew.

And now it was dawn. He rose strong on his feet,
   And strode to his ruin'd camp below the wood ;
He drank the breath of the morning cool and sweet ;
   His murderers round him stood.

Light on the Laspur hills was broadening fast,
   The blood-red snow-peaks chilled to a dazzling
      white ;
He turn'd, and saw the golden circle at last,
   Cut by the eastern height.

" O glorious Life, Who dwellest in earth and sun,
   I have lived, I praise and adore Thee."
                A sword swept.
Over the pass the voices one by one
   Faded, and the hill slept.

Henry Newbolt.

16. ENGLAND

SHALL we but turn from braggart pride
     Our race to cheapen and defame ?
Before the world to wail, to chide,
And weakness as with vaunting claim ?
Ere the hour strikes, to abdicate
The steadfast spirit that made us great,
And rail with scolding tongues at fate ?

If England's heritage indeed
Be lost, be traded quite away
For fatted sloth and fevered greed ;
If, inly rotting, we decay ;
Suffer we then what doom we must,
But silent, as befits the dust
Of them whose chastisement was just.

But rather, England, rally thou
Whatever breathes of faith that still
Within thee keeps the undying vow
And dedicates the constant will.
For such yet lives, if not among
The boasters, or the loud of tongue,
Who cry that England's knell is rung.

The faint of heart, the small of brain,
In thee but their own image find :
Beyond such thoughts as these contain
A mightier Presence is enshrined.
Nor meaner than their birthright grown
Shall these thy latest sons be shown,
So thou but use them for thine own.

By those great spirits burning high
In our home's heaven, that shall be stars
To shine, when all is history
And rumour of old, idle wars ;
By all those hearts which proudly bled
To make this rose of England red ;
The living, the triumphant dead ;

By all who suffered and stood fast
That Freedom might the weak uphold,
And in men's ways of wreck and waste
Justice her awful flower unfold ;
By all who out of grief and wrong
In passion's art of noble song
Made Beauty to our speech belong ;

By those adventurous ones who went
Forth overseas, and, self-exiled,
Sought from far isle and continent
Another England in the wild,
For whom no drums beat, yet they fought
Alone, in courage of a thought
Which an unbounded future wrought ;

Yea, and yet more by those to-day
Who toil and serve for naught of gain,
That in thy purer glory they
May melt their ardour and their pain ;
By these and by the faith of these,
The faith that glorifies and frees,
Thy lands call on thee, and thy seas.

If thou hast sinned, shall we forsake
Thee, or the less account us thine ?
Thy sores, thy shames on us we take.
Flies not for us thy famed ensign ?
Be ours to cleanse and to atone ;
No man this burden bears alone ;
England, our best shall be thine own.

Lift up thy cause into the light !
Put all the factious lips to shame !
Our loves, our faiths, our hopes unite
And strike into a single flame !
Whatever from without betide,
O purify the soul of pride
In us ; thy slumbers cast aside ;
And of thy sons be justified !

Laurence Binyon.

17. THE VOLUNTEER

" **H**E leapt to arms unbidden,
    Unneeded, over-bold ;
His face by earth is hidden,
    His heart in earth is cold.

" Curse on that reckless daring
    That could not wait the call,
The proud fantastic bearing
    That would be first to fall ! "

O tears of human passion,
   Blur not the image true ;
This was not folly's fashion,
   This was the man we knew.
                Henry Newbolt.

18. MANY SISTERS TO MANY BROTHERS

WHEN we fought campaigns (in the long Christmas
    rains)
  With soldiers spread in troops on the floor,
I shot as straight as you, my losses were as few,
  My victories as many, or more.
And when in naval battle, amid cannon's rattle,
  Fleet met fleet in the bath,
My cruisers were as trim, my battleships as grim,
  My submarines cut as swift a path.
Or, when it rained too long, and the strength of the
    strong
  Surged up and broke a way with blows,
I was as fit and keen, my fists hit as clean,
  Your black eye matched my bleeding nose.
Was there a scrap or ploy in which you, the boy,
  Could better me ?   You could not climb higher,
Ride straighter, run as quick (and to smoke made
    you sick)
. . But I sit here, and you're under fire.

Oh, it's you that have the luck, out there in blood
    and muck :
  You were born beneath a kindly star ;

All we dreamt, I and you, you can really go and do,
   And I can't, the way things are.
In a trench you are sitting, while I am knitting
   A hopeless sock that never gets done.
Well, here's luck, my dear ;—and you've got it, no
    fear ;
   But for me . . . a war is poor fun.

                     Rose Macaulay.

19. THE DEFENDERS

HIS wage of rest at nightfall still
   He takes, who sixty years has known
Of ploughing over Cotsall hill
   And keeping trim the Cotsall stone.

He meditates the dusk, and sees
   Folds of his wonted shepherdings
And lands of stubble and tall trees
   Becoming insubstantial things.

And does he see on Cotsall hill—
   Thrown even to the central shire—
The funnelled shapes forbidding still
   The stranger from his cottage fire ?

                   John Drinkwater.

20. THE DEAD

THESE hearts were woven of human joys and cares,
   Washed marvellously with sorrow, swift to mirth.
The years had given them kindness. Dawn was
    theirs,
   And sunset, and the colours of the earth.

These had seen movement, and heard music ; known
  Slumber and waking ; loved ; gone proudly
    friended ;
Felt the quick stir of wonder ; sat alone ;
  Touched flowers and furs and cheeks. All this is
    ended.

There are waters blown by changing winds to laughter
And lit by the rich skies, all day. And after,
  Frost, with a gesture, stays the waves that dance
And wandering loveliness. He leaves a white
  Unbroken glory, a gathered radiance,
A width, a shining peace, under the night.

Rupert Brooke.

21. THE SOLDIER

IF I should die, think only this of me :
  That there's some corner of a foreign field
That is for ever England. There shall be
  In that rich earth a richer dust concealed ;
A dust whom England bore, shaped, made aware,
  Gave, once, her flowers to love, her ways to roam,
A body of England's, breathing English air,
  Washed by the rivers, blest by suns of home.

And think, this heart, all evil shed away,
  A pulse in the eternal mind, no less
    Gives somewhere back the thoughts by England
     given ;
Her sights and sounds ; dreams happy as her day ;
  And laughter, learnt of friends ; and gentleness,
    In hearts at peace, under an English heaven.

Rupert Brooke.

22. FOR THE FALLEN

WITH proud thanksgiving, a mother for her
        children,
England mourns for her dead across the sea.
Flesh of her flesh they were, spirit of her spirit,
Fallen in the cause of the free.

Solemn the drums thrill : Death august and royal
Sings sorrow up into immortal spheres.
There is music in the midst of desolation
And a glory that shines upon our tears.

They went with songs to the battle, they were young,
Straight of limb, true of eye, steady and aglow.
They were staunch to the end against odds uncounted,
They fell with their faces to the foe.

They shall grow not old, as we that are left grow old :
Age shall not weary them, nor the years condemn.
At the going down of the sun and in the morning
We will remember them.

They mingle not with their laughing comrades again ;
They sit no more at familiar tables of home ;
They have no lot in our labour of the day-time :
They sleep beyond England's foam.

But where our desires are and our hopes profound,
Felt as a well-spring that is hidden from sight,
To the innermost heart of their own land they are
        known
As the stars are known to the Night ;

As the stars that shall be bright when we are dust
Moving in marches upon the heavenly plain,
As the stars that are starry in the time of our dark-
    ness,
To the end, to the end, they remain.
                                    Laurence Binyon.

23. SHADOWS AND LIGHTS

WHAT gods have met in battle to arouse
    This whirling shadow of invisible things,
These hosts that writhe amid the shattered sods ?
O Father, and O Mother of the gods,
Is there some trouble in the heavenly house ?
We who are captained by its unseen kings
Wonder what thrones are shaken in the skies,
What powers who held dominion o'er our will
Let fall the sceptre, and what destinies
The younger gods may drive us to fulfil.

Have they not swayed us, earth's invisible lords,
With whispers and with breathings from the dark ?
The very border stones of nations mark
Where silence swallowed some wild prophet's words
That rang but for an instant and were still,
Yet were so burthened with eternity,
They maddened all who heard to work their will,
To raise the lofty temple on the hill,
And many a glittering thicket of keen swords
Flashed out to make one law for land and sea,
That earth might move with heaven in company.

The cities that to myriad beauty grew
Were altars raised unto old gods who died,
And they were sacrificed in ruins to
The younger gods who took their place of pride ;
They have no brotherhood, the deified,
No high companionship of throne by throne,
But will their beauty still to be alone.

What is a nation but a multitude
United by some god-begotten mood,
Some hope of liberty or dream of power
That have not with each other brotherhood
But warred in spirit from their natal hour,
Their hatred god-begotten as their love
Reverberations of eternal strife ?
For all that fury breathed in human life,
Are ye not guilty, answer, ye above ?

Ah, no, the circle of the heavenly ones,
That ring of burning, grave, inflexible powers,
Array in harmony amid the deep
The shining legionaries of the suns,
That through their day from dawn to twilight keep
The peace of heaven, and have no feuds like ours.
The Morning Stars their labours of the dawn
Close at the advent of the Solar Kings,
And these with joy their sceptres yield, withdrawn
When the still Evening Stars begin their reign,
And twilight time is thrilled with homing wings
To the All-Father being turned again.

No, not on high begin divergent ways,
The galaxies of interlinked lights
Rejoicing on each other's beauty gaze,
'Tis we who do make errant all the rays
That stream upon us from the astral heights.
Love in our thickened air too redly burns ;
And unto vanity our beauty turns ;
Wisdom, that gently whispers us to part
From evil, swells to hatred in the heart.
Dark is the shadow of invisible things
On us who look not up, whose vision fails.
The glorious shining of the heavenly kings
To mould us in their image naught avails,
They weave a robe of many-coloured fire
To garb the spirits thronging in the deep,
And in the upper air its splendours keep
Pure and unsullied, but below it trails
Darkling and glimmering in our earthly mire.

With eyes bent ever earthwards we are swayed
But by the shadows of eternal light,
And shadow against shadow is arrayed
So that one dark may dominate the night.
Though kindred are the lights that cast the shade,
We look not up, nor see how, side by side,
The high originals of all our pride
In crowned and sceptred brotherhood are throned,
Compassionate of our blindness and our hate
That own the godship but the love disowned.
Ah, let us for a little while abate
The outward roving eye, and seek within

Where spirit unto spirit is allied ;
There, in our inmost being, we may win
The joyful vision of the heavenly wise
To see the beauty in each other's eyes.

A. E.

24. BRUMANA

OH shall I never never be home again !
    Meadows of England shining in the rain
Spread wide your daisied lawns : your ramparts green
With briar fortify, with blossom screen
Till my far morning—and O streams that slow
And pure and deep through plains and playlands go,
For me your love and all your kingcups store,
And—dark militia of the southern shore,
Old fragrant friends—preserve me the last lines
Of that long saga which you sang me, pines,
When, lonely boy, beneath the chosen tree
I listened, with my eyes upon the sea.

O traitor pines, you sang what life has found
The falsest of fair tales.
Earth blew a far-horn prelude all around,
That native music of her forest home,
While from the sea's blue fields and syren dales
Shadows and light noon spectres of the foam
Riding the summer gales
On aery viols plucked an idle sound.

Hearing you sing, O trees,
Hearing you murmur, " There are older seas,
That beat on vaster sands,

Where the wise snailfish move their pearly towers
To carven rocks and sculptured promont'ries,"
Hearing you whisper, " Lands
Where blaze the unimaginable flowers."

Beneath me in the valley waves the palm,
Beneath, beyond the valley, breaks the sea ;
Beneath me sleep in mist and light and calm
Cities of Lebanon, dream-shadow-dim,
Where Kings of Tyre and Kings of Tyre did rule
In ancient days in endless dynasty,
And all around the snowy mountains swim
Like mighty swans afloat in heaven's pool.

But I will walk upon the wooded hill
Where stands a grove, O pines, of sister pines,
And when the downy twilight droops her wing
And no sea glimmers and no mountain shines
My heart shall listen still.
For pines are gossip pines the wide world through
And full of runic tales to sigh or sing.
'Tis ever sweet through pines to see the sky
Blushing a deeper gold or darker blue.
'Tis ever sweet to lie
On the dry carpet of the needles brown,
And though the fanciful green lizard stir
And windy odours light as thistledown
Breathe from the lavdanon and lavender,
Half to forget the wandering and pain,
Half to remember days that have gone by,
And dream and dream that I am home again !

James Elroy Flecker.

25. A LYKE-WAKE CAROL

G ROW old and die, rich Day,
   Over some English field—
Chartered to come away
   What time to Death you yield !
Pass, frost-white ghost, and then
Come forth to banish'd men !

I see the stubble's sheen,
   The mist and ruddled leaves,
Here where the new Spring's green
   For her first rain-drops grieves.
Here beechen leaves drift red
Last week in England dead.

For English eyes' delight
   Those Autumn ghosts go free—
Ghost of the field hoar-white,
   Ghost of the crimson tree.
Grudge them not, England dear,
To us thy banished here !

Arthur Shearly Cripps.

26. A REFRAIN

T ELL the tune his feet beat
   On the ground all day—
Black-burnt ground and green grass
Seamed with rocks of grey—
" England," " England," " England,"
That one word they say.

Now they tread the beech-mast,
Now the ploughland's clay,
Now the faëry ball-floor of her fields in May.
Now her red June sorrel, now her new-turned hay,
Now they keep the great road, now by sheep-path
    stray,
Still it's " England," " England,"
" England " all the way !

Arthur Shearly Cripps.

27. WHERE A ROMAN VILLA STOOD, ABOVE FREIBURG

ON alien ground, breathing an alien air,
    A Roman stood, far from his ancient home,
And gazing, murmured, " Ah, the hills are fair,
    But not the hills of Rome ! "

Descendant of a race to Romans kin,
    Where the old son of Empire stood, I stand.
The self-same rocks fold the same valley in,
    Untouched of human hand.

Over another shines the self-same star,
    Another heart with nameless longing fills,
Crying aloud, " How beautiful they are,
    But not our English hills ! "

Mary E. Coleridge.

28. HEIGHTS AND DEPTHS

H E walked in glory on the hills ;
　　We dalesmen envied from afar
The heights and rose-lit pinnacles
　　Which placed him nigh the evening star.

Upon the peaks they found him dead ;
　　And now we wonder if he sighed
For our low grass beneath his head,
　　For our rude huts, before he died.

William Canton.

29. IN THE HIGHLANDS

I N the highlands, in the country places,
　　Where the old plain men have rosy faces,
　　And the young fair maidens
　　　　Quiet eyes ;
Where essential silence cheers and blesses,
And for ever in the hill-recesses
　　Her more lovely music
　　　　Broods and dies.

O to mount again where erst I haunted ;
Where the old red hills are bird-enchanted,
　　And the low green meadows
　　　　Bright with sward ;
And when even dies, the million-tinted,
And the night has come, and planets glinted,
　　Lo, the valley hollow
　　　　Lamp-bestarred !

O to dream, O to awake and wander
There, and with delight to take and render,
   Through the trance of silence,
     Quiet breath ;
Lo ! for there, among the flowers and grasses,
Only the mightier movement sounds and passes ;
   Only winds and rivers,
     Life and death.

Robert Louis Stevenson.

30. IN CITY STREETS

YONDER in the heather there's a bed for sleeping,
   Drink for one athirst, ripe blackberries to eat ;
Yonder in the sun the merry hares go leaping,
   And the pool is clear for travel-wearied feet.

Sorely throb my feet, a-tramping London highways,
   (Ah ! the springy moss upon a northern moor !)
Through the endless streets, the gloomy squares and
     byways,
   Homeless in the City, poor among the poor !

London streets are gold—ah, give me leaves a-glinting
   'Midst grey dykes and hedges in the autumn sun !
London water's wine, poured out for all unstinting—
   God ! For the little brooks that tumble as they run !

Oh, my heart is fain to hear the soft wind blowing,
   Soughing through the fir-tops up on northern fells !
Oh, my eye's an ache to see the brown burns flowing
   Through the peaty soil and tinkling heather-bells.

Ada Smith.

31. MARGARET'S SONG

Too soothe and mild your lowland airs
　　For one whose hope is gone :
I'm thinking of a little tarn,
　　Brown, very lone.

Would now the tall swift mists could lay
　　Their wet grasp on my hair,
And the great natures of the hills
　　Round me friendly were.

In vain !—For taking hills your plains
　　Have spoilt my soul, I think,
But would my feet were going down
　　Towards the brown tarn's brink.

Lascelles Abercrombie.

32. TO S. R. CROCKETT

Blows the wind to-day, and the sun and the rain
　　are flying,
　Blows the wind on the moors to-day and now,
Where about the graves of the martyrs the whaups are
　　crying,
　My heart remembers how !

Grey recumbent tombs of the dead in desert places,
　　Standing stones on the vacant wine-red moor,
Hills of sheep, and the howes of the silent vanishea
　　races,
　And winds, austere and pure :

Be it granted me to behold you again in dying,
    Hills of home ! and to hear again the call ;
Hear about the graves of the martyrs the peewees
        crying,
    And hear no more at all.

Robert Louis Stevenson.

33. CHILLINGHAM

I

THROUGH the sunny garden
        The humming bees are still ;
The fir climbs the heather,
    The heather climbs the hill.

The low clouds have riven
    A little rift through.
The hill climbs to heaven,
    Far away and blue.

II

O the high valley, the little low hill,
    And the cornfield over the sea,
The wind that rages and then lies still,
    And the clouds that rest and flee !

O the gray island in the rainbow haze,
    And the long thin spits of land,
The roughening pastures and the stony ways,
    And the golden flash of the sand !

O the red heather on the moss-wrought rock,
    And the fir-tree stiff and straight,
The shaggy old sheep-dog barking at the flock,
    And the rotten old five-barred gate !

O the brown bracken, the blackberry bough,
    The scent of the gorse in the air !
I shall love them ever as I love them now,
    I shall weary in Heaven to be there !

III

Strike, Life, a happy hour, and let me live
    But in that grace !
I shall have gathered all the world can give,
    Unending Time and Space !

Bring light and air—the thin and shining air
    Of the North land,
The light that falls on tower and garden there,
    Close to the gold sea-sand.

Bring flowers, the latest colours of the earth,
    Ere nun-like frost
Lay her hard hand upon this rainbow mirth,
    With twinkling emerald crossed.

The white star of the traveller's joy, the deep
    Empurpled rays that hide the smoky stone,
The dahlia rooted in Egyptian sleep,
    The last frail rose alone.

Let music whisper from a casement set
　　By them of old,
Where the light smell of lavender may yet
　　Rise from the soft loose mould.

Then shall I know, with eyes and ears awake,
　　Not in bright gleams,
The joy my Heavenly Father joys to make
　　For men who grieve, in dreams !

　　　　　　　　　Mary E. Coleridge.

34. SUSSEX

G OD gave all men all earth to love,
　　But since our hearts are small,
Ordained for each one spot should prove
　　Beloved over all ;
That as He watched Creation's birth
　　So we, in godlike mood,
May of our love create our earth
　　And see that it is good.

So one shall Baltic pines content,
　　As one some Surrey glade,
Or one the palm-grove's droned lament
　　Before Levuka's trade.
Each to his choice, and I rejoice
　　The lot has fallen to me
In a fair ground—in a fair ground—
　　Yea, Sussex by the sea !

No tender-hearted garden crowns,
   No bosomed woods adorn
Our blunt, bow-headed, whale-backed Downs,
   But gnarled and writhen thorn—
Bare slopes where chasing shadows skim,
   And through the gaps revealed
Belt upon belt, the wooded, dim
   Blue goodness of the Weald.

Clean of officious fence or hedge,
   Half-wild and wholly tame,
The wise turf cloaks the white cliff edge
   As when the Romans came.
What sign of those that fought and died
   At shift of sword and sword ?
The barrow and the camp abide,
   The sunlight and the sward.

Here leaps ashore the full Sou'west
   All heavy-winged with brine,
Here lies above the folded crest
   The Channel's leaden line ;
And here the sea-fogs lap and cling,
   And here, each warning each,
The sheep-bells and the ship-bells ring
   Along the hidden beach.

We have no waters to delight
   Our broad and brookless vales—
Only the dewpond on the height
   Unfed, that never fails,

Whereby no tattered herbage tells
    Which way the season flies—
Only our close-bit thyme that smells
    Like dawn in Paradise.

Here through the strong unhampered days
    The tinkling silence thrills ;
Or little, lost, Down churches praise
    The Lord who made the hills :
But here the Old Gods guard their round,
    And, in her secret heart,
The heathen kingdom Wilfrid found
    Dreams, as she dwells, apart.

Though all the rest were all my share,
    With equal soul I'd see
Her nine-and-thirty sisters fair,
    Yet none more fair than she.
Choose ye your need from Thames to Tweed,
    And I will choose instead
Such lands as lie 'twixt Rake and Rye,
    Black Down and Beachy Head.

I will go out against the sun
    Where the rolled scarp retires,
And the Long Man of Wilmington
    Looks naked toward the shires ;
And east till doubling Rother crawls
    To find the fickle tide,
By dry and sea-forgotten walls,
    Our ports of stranded pride.

I will go north about the shaws
   And the deep ghylls that breed
Huge oaks and old, the which we hold
   No more than " Sussex weed " ;
Or south where windy Piddinghoe's
   Begilded dolphin veers,
And black beside wide-bankèd Ouse
   Lie down our Sussex steers.

So to the land our hearts we give
   Till the sure magic strike,
And Memory, Use, and Love make live
   Us and our fields alike—
That deeper than our speech and thought,
   Beyond our reason's sway,
Clay of the pit whence we were wrought
   Yearns to its fellow-clay.

God gives all men all earth to love,
   But since man's heart is small
Ordains for each one spot shall prove
   Beloved over all.
Each to his choice, and I rejoice
   The lot has fallen to me
In a fair ground—in a fair ground—
   Yea, Sussex by the sea !

Rudyard Kipling.

35. THE SOUTH COUNTRY

WHEN I am living in the Midlands,
   That are sodden and unkind,
I light my lamp in the evening :
   My work is left behind ;
And the great hills of the South Country
   Come back into my mind.

The great hills of the South Country
   They stand along the sea,
And it's there, walking in the high woods,
   That I could wish to be,
And the men that were boys when I was a boy
   Walking along with me.

The men that live in North England
   I saw them for a day :
Their hearts are set upon the waste fells,
   Their skies are fast and grey ;
From their castle-walls a man may see
   The mountains far away.

The men that live in West England
   They see the Severn strong,
A-rolling on rough water brown
   Light aspen leaves along.
They have the secret of the Rocks,
   And the oldest kind of song.

But the men that live in the South Country
   Are the kindest and most wise,
They get their laughter from the loud surf,
   And the faith in their happy eyes

Comes surely from our Sister the Spring
    When over the sea she flies ;
The violets suddenly bloom at her feet,
    She blesses us with surprise.

I never get between the pines
    But I smell the Sussex air ;
Nor I never come on a belt of sand
    But my home is there.
And along the sky the line of the Downs
    So noble and so bare.

A lost thing could I never find,
    Nor a broken thing mend :
And I fear I shall be all alone
    When I get towards the end,
Who will there be to comfort me
    Or who will be my friend ?

I will gather and carefully make my friends
    Of the men of the Sussex Weald,
They watch the stars from silent folds,
    They stiffly plough the field.
By them and the God of the South Country
    My poor soul shall be healed.

If I ever become a rich man,
    Or if ever I grow to be old,
I will build a house with deep thatch
    To shelter me from the cold,
And there shall the Sussex songs be sung
    And the story of Sussex told.

I will hold my house in the high wood,
 Within a walk of the sea,
And the men that were boys when I was a boy
 Shall sit and drink with me.

     Hilaire Belloc.

36. CHANCLEBURY RING

SAY what you will, there is not in the world
 A nobler sight than from this upper down.
No rugged landscape here, no beauty hurled
From its Creator's hand as with a frown ;
But a green plain on which green hills look down
Trim as a garden plot. No other hue
Can hence be seen, save here and there the brown
Of a square fallow, and the horizon's blue.
Dear checker-work of woods, the Sussex weald,
If a name thrills me yet of things of earth,
That name is thine ! How often I have fled
To thy deep hedgerows and embraced each field,
Each lag, each pasture,—fields which gave me birth
And saw my youth, and which must hold me dead.

     Wilfrid Blunt.

37. IN ROMNEY MARSH

As I went down to Dymchurch Wall,
 I heard the South sing o'er the land ;
I saw the yellow sunlight fall
 On knolls where Norman churches stand.

And ringing shrilly, taut and lithe,
    Within the wind a core of sound,
The wire from Romney town to Hythe
    Along its airy journey wound.

A veil of purple vapour flowed
    And trailed its fringe along the Straits;
The upper air like sapphire glowed;
    And roses filled Heaven's central gates.

Masts in the offing wagged their tops;
    The swinging waves pealed on the shore;
The saffron beach, all diamond drops
    And beads of surge, prolonged the roar.

As I came up from Dymchurch Wall,
    I saw above the Down's low crest
The crimson brands of sunset fall,
    Flicker and fade from out the west.

Night sank: like flakes of silver fire
    The stars in one great shower came down;
Shrill blew the wind; and shrill the wire
    Rang out from Hythe to Romney town.

The darkly shining salt sea drops
    Streamed as the waves clashed on the shore;
The beach, with all its organ stops
    Pealing again, prolonged the roar.
                       John Davidson.

38. A CINQUE PORT

BELOW the down the stranded town
  What may betide forlornly waits,
With memories of smoky skies,
  When Gallic navies crossed the straits ;
When waves with fire and blood grew bright,
And cannon thundered through the night.

With swinging stride the rhythmic tide
  Bore to the harbour barque and sloop ;
Across the bar the ship of war,
  In castled stern and lanterned poop,
Came up with conquests on her lee,
The stately mistress of the sea.

Where argosies have wooed the breeze,
  The simple sheep are feeding now ;
And near and far across the bar
  The ploughman whistles at the plough ;
Where once the long waves washed the shore,
Larks from their lowly lodgings soar.

Below the down the stranded town
  Hears far away the rollers beat ;
About the wall the seabirds call ;
  The salt wind murmurs through the street ;
Forlorn the sea's forsaken bride
Awaits the end that shall betide.

John Davidson.

39. ESSEX

I GO through the fields of blue water
  On the South road of the sea.
High to North the East-Country
  Holds her green fields to me—
For she that I gave over,
  Gives not over me.

Last night I lay at Good Easter
  Under a hedge I knew,
Last night beyond High Easter
  I trod the May-floors blue—
Till from the sea the sun came
  Bidding me wake and rue.

Roding (that names eight churches)—
  Banks with the paigles dight—
Chelmer whose mill and willows
  Keep one red tower in sight—
Under the Southern Cross run
  Beside the ship to-night.

Ah ! I may not seek back now,
  Neither be turned nor stayed.
Yet should I live, I'd seek her,
  Once that my vows are paid !
And should I die I'd haunt her—
  I being what God made !

England has greater counties—
  Their peace to hers is small.

Low hills, rich fields, calm rivers,
    In Essex seek them all,—
Essex, where I that found them
    Found to lose them all!
                    Arthur Shearly Cripps.

40. A TOWN WINDOW

BEYOND my window in the night
    Is but a drab inglorious street,
Yet there the frost and clean starlight
    As over Warwick woods are sweet.

Under the grey drift of the town
    The crocus works among the mould
As eagerly as those that crown
    The Warwick spring in flame and gold.

And when the tramway down the hill
    Across the cobbles moans and rings,
There is about my window-sill
    The tumult of a thousand wings.
                    John Drinkwater.

41. MAMBLE

I NEVER went to Mamble
    That lies above the Teme,
So I wonder who's in Mamble,
    And whether people seem
Who breed and brew along there
    As lazy as the name,
And whether any song there
    Sets alehouse wits aflame.

110278

The finger-post says Mamble,
    And that is all I know
Of the narrow road to Mamble,
    And should I turn and go
To that place of lazy token,
    That lies above the Teme,
There might be a Mamble broken
    That was lissom in a dream.

So leave the road to Mamble
    And take another road
To as good a place as Mamble
    Be it lazy as a toad ;
Who travels Worcester county
    Takes any place that comes
When April tosses bounty
    To the cherries and the plums.

                        John Drinkwater.

42. PLYMOUTH HARBOUR

OH, what know they of harbours
    Who toss not on the sea !
They tell of fairer havens,
    But none so fair there be

As Plymouth town outstretching
    Her quiet arms to me ;
Her breast's broad welcome spreading
    From Mewstone to Penlee.

Ah, with this home-thought, darling,
    Come crowding thoughts of thee.
Oh, what know they of harbours
    Who toss not on the sea !

Ernest Radford.

43. OXFORD

I CAME to Oxford in the light
    Of a spring-coloured afternoon ;
Some clouds were grey and some were white,
    And all were blown to such a tune
Of quiet rapture in the sky,
I laughed to see them laughing by.

I had been dreaming in the train
    With thoughts at random from my book ;
I looked, and read, and looked again,
    And suddenly to greet my look
Oxford shone up with every tower
Aspiring sweetly like a flower.

Home turn the feet of men that seek,
    And home the hearts of children turn,
And none can teach the hour to speak
    What every hour is free to learn ;
And all discover, late or soon,
Their golden Oxford afternoon.

44. ALMA MATER

K NOW you her secret none can utter ?
      Hers of the Book, the tripled Crown ?
Still on the spire the pigeons flutter,
    Still by the gateway flits the gown ;
Still on the street, from corbel and gutter,
    Faces of stone look down.

Faces of stone, and stonier faces—
    Some from library windows wan
Forth on her gardens, her green spaces,
    Peer and turn to their books anon.
Hence, my Muse, from the green oases
    Gather the tent, begone !

Nay, should she by the pavement linger
    Under the rooms where once she played,
Who from the feast would rise to fling her
    One poor *sou* for her serenade ?
One short laugh for the antic finger
    Thrumming a lute-string frayed ?

Once, my dear—but the world was young then—
    Magdalen elms and Trinity limes—
Lissom the blades and the backs that swung then,
    Eight good men in the good old times—
Careless we, and the chorus flung then
    Under St. Mary's chimes !

Reins lay loose and the ways led random—
    Christ Church meadow and Iffley track,

" Idleness horrid and dog-cart " (tandem),
　　Aylesbury grind and Bicester pack—
Pleasant our lines, and faith ! we scanned 'em ;
　　Having that artless knack.

Come, old limmer, the times grow colder ;
　　Leaves of the creeper redden and fall.
Was it a hand then clapped my shoulder ?—
　　Only the wind by the chapel wall !
Dead leaves drift on the lute . . . So fold her
　　Under the faded shawl.

Never we wince, though none deplore us,
　　We who go reaping that we sowed ;
Cities at cockcrow wake before us—
　　Hey, for the lilt of the London road !
One look back, and a rousing chorus !
　　Never a palinode !

Still on her spire the pigeons hover ;
　　Still by her gateway haunts the gown.
Ah, but her secret ?　You, young lover,
　　Drumming her old ones forth from town,
Know you the secret none discover ?
　　Tell it—when *you* go down.

Yet if at length you seek her, prove her,
　　Lean to her whispers never so nigh ;
Yet if at last not less her lover
　　You in your hansom leave the High ;
Down from her towers a ray shall hover—
　　Touch you, a passer-by.
　　　　　　　　　　Arthur Quiller-Couch.

45. FROM "DEDICATORY ODE"

I WILL not try the reach again,
   I will not set my sail alone,
To moor a boat bereft of men
   At Yarnton's tiny docks of stone.

But I will sit beside the fire,
   And put my hand before my eyes,
And trace, to fill my heart's desire,
   The last of all our Odysseys.

The quiet evening kept her tryst :
   Beneath an open sky we rode,
And passed into a wandering mist
   Along the perfect Evenlode.

The tender Evenlode that makes
   Her meadows hush to hear the sound
Of waters mingling in the brakes,
   And binds my heart to English ground.

A lovely river, all alone,
   She lingers in the hills and holds
A hundred little towns of stone,
   Forgotten in the western wolds.

Hilaire Belloc.

46. THE DEVOURERS

CAMBRIDGE town is a beleaguered city ;
   For south and north, like a sea,
There beat on its gates, without haste or pity,
   The downs and the fen country.

Cambridge towers, so old, so wise,
    They were builded but yesterday,
Watched by sleepy gray secret eyes
    That smiled as at children's play.

Roads south of Cambridge run into the waste,
    Where learning and lamps are not,
And the pale downs tumble, blind, chalk-faced,
    And the brooding churches squat.

Roads north of Cambridge march through a plain
    Level like the traitor sea.
It will swallow its ships, and turn and smile again—
    The insatiable fen country.

Lest the downs and the fens should eat Cambridge up,
    And its towers be tossed and thrown,
And its rich wine drunk from its broken cup,
    And its beauty no more known—

Let us come, you and I, where the roads run blind,
    Out beyond the transient city,
That our love, mingling with earth, may find
    Her imperishable heart of pity.
                                    Rose Macaulay.

47. THE OLD VICARAGE, GRANTCHESTER

Café des Westens, Berlin

JUST now the lilac is in bloom,
        All before my little room ;
And in my flower-beds, I think,

Smile the carnation and the pink ;
And down the borders, well I know,
The poppy and the pansy blow . . .
Oh ! there the chestnuts, summer through,
Beside the river make for you
A tunnel of green gloom, and sleep
Deeply above ; and green and deep
The stream mysterious glides beneath,
Green as a dream and deep as death.—
Oh, damn ! I know it ! and I know
How the May fields all golden show,
And when the day is young and sweet,
Gild gloriously the bare feet
That run to bathe . . .
                    Du lieber Gott !

Here am I, sweating, sick, and hot,
And there the shadowed waters fresh
Lean up to embrace the naked flesh.
Temperamentvoll German Jews
Drink beer around ; and *there* the dews
Are soft beneath a morn of gold.
Here tulips bloom as they are told ;
Unkempt about those hedges blows
An English unofficial rose ;
And there the unregulated sun
Slopes down to rest when day is done,
And wakes a vague unpunctual star,
A slippered Hesper ; and there are
Meads towards Haslingfield and Coton
Where *das Betreten*'s not *verboten*. . .

εἴθε γενοίμην . . . would I were
In Grantchester, in Grantchester !—
Some, it may be, can get in touch
With Nature there, or Earth, or such.
And clever modern men have seen
A Faun a-peeping through the green,
And felt the Classics were not dead,
To glimpse a Naiad's reedy head,
Or hear the Goat-foot piping low . . .
But these are things I do not know.
I only know that you may lie
Day long and watch the Cambridge sky,
And, flower-lulled in sleepy grass,
Hear the cool lapse of hours pass,
Until the centuries blend and blur
In Grantchester, in Grantchester . . .
Still in the dawnlit waters cool
His ghostly Lordship swims his pool,
And tries the strokes, essays the tricks,
Long learnt on Hellespont, or Styx ;
Dan Chaucer hears his river still
Chatter beneath a phantom mill ;
Tennyson notes, with studious eye,
How Cambridge waters hurry by . . .
And in that garden, black and white
Creep whispers through the grass all night ;
And spectral dance, before the dawn,
A hundred Vicars down the lawn ;
Curates, long dust, will come and go
On lissom, clerical, printless toe ;
And oft between the boughs is seen

The sly shade of a Rural Dean . . .
Till, at a shiver in the skies,
Vanishing with Satanic cries,
The prim ecclesiastic rout
Leaves but a startled sleeper-out,
Grey heavens, the first bird's drowsy calls,
The falling house that never falls.

God ! I will pack, and take a train,
And get me to England once again !
For England's the one land, I know,
Where men with Splendid Hearts may go ;
And Cambridgeshire, of all England,
The shire for Men who Understand ;
And of *that* district I prefer
The lovely hamlet Grantchester.
For Cambridge people rarely smile,
Being urban, squat, and packed with guile ;
And Royston men in the far South
Are black and fierce and strange of mouth ;
At Over they fling oaths at one,
And worse than oaths at Trumpington,
And Ditton girls are mean and dirty,
And there's none in Harston under thirty,
And folks in Shelford and those parts,
Have twisted lips and twisted hearts,
And Barton men make cockney rhymes,
And Coton's full of nameless crimes,
And things are done you'd not believe
At Madingley on Christmas Eve.
Strong men have run for miles and miles

When one from Cherry Hinton smiles;
Strong men have blanched and shot their wives
Rather than send them to St. Ives;
Strong men have cried like babes, bydam,
To hear what happened at Babraham.
But Grantchester! ah, Grantchester!
There's peace and holy quiet there,
Great clouds along pacific skies,
And men and women with straight eyes.
Lithe children lovelier than a dream,
A bosky wood, a slumbrous stream,
And little kindly winds that creep
Round twilight corners, half asleep.
In Grantchester their skins are white,
They bathe by day, they bathe by night;
The women there do all they ought;
The men observe the Rules of Thought.
They love the Good; they worship Truth;
They laugh uproariously in youth;
(And when they get to feeling old,
They up and shoot themselves, I'm told). .

Ah God! to see the branches stir
Across the moon at Grantchester!
To smell the thrilling-sweet and rotten
Unforgettable, unforgotten
River smell, and hear the breeze
Sobbing in the little trees.
Say, do the elm-clumps greatly stand,
Still guardians of that holy land?
The chestnuts shade, in reverend dream,

The yet unacademic stream ?
Is dawn a secret shy and cold
Anadyomene, silver-gold ?
And sunset still a golden sea
From Haslingfield to Madingley ?
And after, ere the night is born,
Do hares come out about the corn ?
Oh, is the water sweet and cool
Gentle and brown, above the pool ?
And laughs the immortal river still
Under the mill, under the mill ?
Say, is there Beauty yet to find ?
And Certainty ? and Quiet kind ?
Deep meadows yet, for to forget
The lies, and truths, and pain ? . . . oh ! yet
Stands the Church clock at ten to three ?
And is there honey still for tea ?

Rupert Brooke.

48. DAYS THAT HAVE BEEN

CAN I forget the sweet days that have been,
    When poetry first began to warm my blood ;
When from the hills of Gwent I saw the earth
    Burned into two by Severn's silver flood :

When I would go alone at night to see
    The moonlight, like a big white butterfly,
Dreaming on that old castle near Caerleon,
    While at its side the Usk went softly by :

When I would stare at lovely clouds in Heaven,
  Or watch them when reported by deep streams ;
When feeling pressed like thunder, but would not
  Break into that grand music of my dreams ?

Can I forget the sweet days that have been,
  The villages so green I have been in ;
Llantarnam, Magor, Malpas, and Llanwern,
  Liswery, old Caerleon, and Alteryn ?

Can I forget the banks of Malpas Brook,
  Or Ebbw's voice in such a wild delight,
As on he dashed with pebbles in his throat,
  Gurgling towards the sea with all his might ?

Ah, when I see a leafy village now
  I sigh and ask it for Llantarnam's green ;
I ask each river where is Ebbw's voice—
  In memory of the sweet days that have been.
                                William H. Davies.

49. THE LAKE ISLE OF INNISFREE

I will arise and go now, and go to Innisfree,
  And a small cabin build there, of clay and
    wattles made ;
Nine bean rows will I have there, a hive for the honey
  bee,
And live alone in the bee-loud glade.

And I shall have some peace there, for peace comes
    dropping slow,
Dropping from the veils of the morning to where the
    cricket sings ;
There midnight's all a glimmer, and noon a purple
    glow,
And evening full of the linnet's wings.

I will arise and go now, for always night and day
I hear lake water lapping with low sounds by the
    shore ;
While I stand on the roadway, or on the pavements
    gray,
I hear it in the deep heart's core.

W. B. Yeats.

50. THE FLOWERS

*B*UY *my English posies !*
    Kent and Surrey may—
Violets of the Undercliff
    Wet with Channel spray ;
Cowslips from a Devon combe—
    Midland furze afire—
Buy my English posies,
    And I'll sell your heart's desire !

Buy my English posies !
    You that scorn the may,
Won't you greet a friend from home
    Half the world away ?

Green against the draggled drift,
    Faint and frail and first—
Buy my Northern blood-root
    And I'll know where you were nursed .

Robin down the logging-road whistles, " Come to
    me ! "
Spring has found the maple-grove, the sap is running
    free ;
All the winds of Canada call the ploughing-rain.
Take the flower and turn the hour, and kiss your love
    again !

    Buy my English posies !
        Here's to match your need—
    Buy a tuft of royal heath,
        Buy a bunch of weed
    White as sand of Muysenberg
        Spun before the gale—
    Buy my heath and lilies
        And I'll tell you whence you hail !

Under hot Constantia broad the vineyards lie—
Throned and thorned the aching berg props the speck-
    less sky—
Slow below the Wynberg firs trails the tilted wain—
Take the flower and turn the hour, and kiss your love
    again.

    Buy my English posies !
        You that will not turn—
    Buy my hot-wood clematis,
        Buy a frond o' fern

Gather'd where the Erskine leaps
　　Down the road to Lorne—
Buy my Christmas creeper
　　And I'll say where you were born !

West away from Melbourne dust holidays begin—
They that mock at Paradise woo at Cora Lynn—
Through the great South Otway gums sings the great
　　South Main—
Take the flower and turn the hour, and kiss your love
　　again.

　　Buy my English posies !
　　　　Here's your choice unsold !
　　Buy a blood-red myrtle-bloom,
　　　　Buy the kowhai's gold
　　Flung for gift on Taupo's face,
　　　　Sign that spring is come—
　　Buy my clinging myrtle
　　　　And I'll give you back your home !

Broom behind the windy town ; pollen o' the pine—
Bell-bird in the leafy deep where the *ratas* twine—
Fern above the saddle-bow, flax upon the plain—
Take the flower and turn the hour, and kiss your love
　　again.

　　Buy my English posies !
　　　　Ye that have your own
　　Buy them for a brother's sake
　　　　Overseas, alone.

Weed ye trample underfoot
Floods his heart abrim—
Bird ye never heeded,
O, she calls his dead to him.

Far and far our homes are set round the Seven Seas ;
Woe for us if we forget, we that hold by these !
Unto each his mother-beach, bloom and bird and
land—
Masters of the Seven Seas, oh, love and understand.

Rudyard Kipling.

51. THE HOUSE BEAUTIFUL

A NAKED house, a naked moor,
  A shivering pool before the door,
A garden bare of flowers and fruit
And poplars at the garden foot :
Such is the place that I live in,
Bleak without and bare within.

Yet shall your ragged moor receive
The incomparable pomp of eve,
And the cold glories of the dawn
Behind your shivering trees be drawn ;
And when the wind from place to place
Doth the unmoored cloud-galleons chase,
Your garden gloom and gleam again,
With leaping sun, with glancing rain.
Here shall the wizard moon ascend
The heavens, in the crimson end

Of day's declining splendour ; here
The army of the stars appear.
The neighbour hollows dry or wet,
Spring shall with tender flowers beset ;
And oft the morning muser see
Larks rising from the broomy lea,
And every fairy wheel and thread
Of cobweb dew-bediamonded.
When daisies go, shall winter time
Silver the simple grass with rime ;
Autumnal frosts enchant the pool
And make the cart-ruts beautiful ;
And when snow-bright the moor expands,
How shall your children clap their hands !
To make this earth our heritage,
A cheerful and a changeful page,
God's bright and intricate device
Of days and seasons doth suffice.

Robert Louis Stevenson.

52. THE OLD LOVE

OUT of my door I step into
    The country, all her scent and dew,
Nor travel there by a hard road,
Dusty and far from my abode.

The country washes to my door
Green miles on miles in soft uproar,
The thunder of the woods, and then
The backwash of green surf again.

Beyond the feverfew and stocks,
The guelder-rose and hollyhocks ;
Outside my trellised porch a tree
Of lilac frames a sky for me.

A stretch of primrose and pale green
To hold the tender Hesper in ;
Hesper that by the moon makes pale
Her silver keel and silver sail.

The country silence wraps me quite,
Silence and song and pure delight ;
The country beckons all the day
Smiling, and but a step away.

This is that country seen across
How many a league of love and loss,
Prayed for and longed for, and as far
As fountains in the desert are.

This is that country at my door,
Whose fragrant airs run on before,
And call me when the first birds stir
In the green wood to walk with her.

Katharine Tynan.

53. EARLY MORN

WHEN I did wake this morn from sleep,
    It seemed I heard birds in a dream ;
Then I arose to take the air—
    The lovely air that made birds scream ;
Just as a green hill launched the ship
Of gold, to take its first clear dip.

And it began its journey then,
  As I came forth to take the air ;
The timid Stars had vanished quite,
  The Moon was dying with a stare ;
Horses, and kine, and sheep were seen,
As still as pictures, in fields green.

It seemed as though I had surprised
  And trespassed in a golden world
That should have passed while men still slept !
  The joyful birds, the ship of gold,
The horses, kine, and sheep did seem
As they would vanish for a dream.

William H. Davies.

54. THE HILL PINES WERE SIGHING

THE hill pines were sighing,
    O'ercast and chill was the day :
A mist in the valley lying
Blotted the pleasant May.

But deep in the glen's bosom
Summer slept in the fire
Of the odorous gorse-blossom
And the hot scent of the brier.

A ribald cuckoo clamoured,
And out of the copse the stroke
Of the iron axe that hammered
The iron heart of the oak.

Anon a sound appalling,
As a hundred years of pride
Crashed, in the silence falling :
And the shadowy pine-trees sighed.

Robert Bridges.

55. THE CHOICE

WHEN skies are blue and days are bright
A kitchen-garden's my delight,
Set round with rows of decent box
And blowsy girls of hollyhocks.

Before the lark his Lauds hath done
And ere the corncrake's southward gone ;
Before the thrush good-night hath said
And the young Summer's put to bed.

The currant-bushes' spicy smell,
Homely and honest, likes me well,
The while on strawberries I feast,
And raspberries the sun hath kissed.

Beans all a-blowing by a row
Of hives that great with honey go,
With mignonette and heaths to yield
The plundering bee his honey-field.

Sweet herbs in plenty, blue borage
And the delicious mint and sage,
Rosemary, marjoram, and rue,
And thyme to scent the winter through.

Here are small apples growing round,
And apricots all golden-gowned,
And plums that presently will flush
And show their bush a Burning Bush.

Cherries in nets against the wall,
Where Master Thrush his madrigal
Sings, and makes oath a churl is he
Who grudges cherries for a fee.

Lavender, sweet-briar, orris.   Here
Shall Beauty make her pomander,
Her sweet-balls for to lay in clothes
That wrap her as the leaves the rose.

Take roses red and lilies white,
A kitchen garden's my delight ;
Its gillyflowers and phlox and cloves,
And its tall cote of irised doves.
                              Katharine Tynan.

56. THERE IS A HILL

THERE is a hill beside the silver Thames,
    Shady with birch and beech and odorous pine :
And brilliant underfoot with thousand gems
Steeply the thickets to his floods decline.
        Straight trees in every place
        Their thick tops interlace,
And pendent branches trail their foliage fine
        Upon his watery face.

Swift from the sweltering pasturage he flows :
His stream, alert to seek the pleasant shade,
Pictures his gentle purpose, as he goes
Straight to the caverned pool his toil has made.
    His winter floods lay bare
    The stout roots in the air :
His summer streams are cool, when they have played
    Among their fibrous hair.

A rushy island guards the sacred bower,
And hides it from the meadow, where in peace
The lazy cows wrench many a scented flower,
Robbing the golden market of the bees :
    And laden barges float
    By banks of myosote ;
And scented flag and golden flower-de-lys
    Delay the loitering boat.

And on this side the island, where the pool
Eddies away, are tangled mass on mass
The water-weeds, that net the fishes cool,
And scarce allow a narrow stream to pass ;
    Where spreading crowfoot mars
    The drowning nenuphars,
Waving the tassels of her silken grass
    Below her silver stars.

But in the purple pool there nothing grows,
Not the white water-lily spoked with gold ;

Though best she loves the hollows, and well knows
On quiet streams her broad shields to unfold :
    Yet should her roots but try
    Within these deeps to lie,
Not her long-reaching stalk could ever hold
    Her waxen head so high.

Sometimes an angler comes, and drops his hook
Within its hidden depths, and 'gainst a tree
Leaning his rod, reads in some pleasant book,
Forgetting soon his pride of fishery ;
    And dreams, or falls asleep,
    While curious fishes peep
About his nibbled bait, or scornfully
    Dart off and rise and leap.

And sometimes a slow figure 'neath the trees,
In ancient-fashioned smock, with tottering care
Upon a staff propping his weary knees,
May by the pathway of the forest fare :
    As from a buried day
    Across the mind will stray
Some perishing mute shadow,—and unaware
    He passeth on his way.

Else, he that wishes solitude is safe,
Whether he bathe at morning in the stream :
Or lead his love there when the hot hours chafe
The meadows, busy with a blurring stream
    Or watch, as fades the light,
    The gibbous moon grow bright,
Until her magic rays dance in a dream,
    And glorify the night.

Where is this bower beside the silver Thames ?
O pool and flowery thickets, hear my vow !
O trees of freshest foliage and straight stems,
No sharer of my secret I allow :
  Lest ere I come the while
  Strange feet your shades defile ;
Or lest the burly oarsman turn his prow
  Within your guardian isle.

       Robert Bridges.

57. BAB-LOCK-HYTHE

IN the time of wild roses
 As up Thames we travelled
Where 'mid water-weeds ravelled
The lily uncloses,

To his old shores the river
A new song was singing,
And young shoots were springing
On old roots for ever.

Dog-daisies were dancing,
And flags flamed in cluster,
On the dark stream a lustre
Now blurred and now glancing.

A tall reed down-weighing
The sedge-warbler fluttered ;
One sweet note he uttered,
Then left it soft-swaying.

By the bank's sandy hollow
My dipt oars went beating,
And past our bows fleeting
Blue-backed shone the swallow.

High woods, heron-haunted,
Rose, changed, as we rounded
Old hills greenly mounded,
To meadows enchanted.

A dream ever moulded
Afresh for our wonder,
Still opening asunder
For the stream many-folded ;

Till sunset was rimming
The West with pale flushes ;
Behind the black rushes
The last light was dimming ;

And the lonely stream, hiding
Shy birds, grew more lonely,
And with us was only
The noise of our gliding.

In cloud of gray weather
The evening o'erdarkened,
In the stillness we hearkened ;
Our hearts sang together.

Laurence Binyon.

58. ROWER'S CHANT

R ow till the land dip 'neath
　　The sea from view.
Row till a land peep up,
A home for you.

Row till the mast sing songs
Welcome and sweet.
Row till the waves, out-stripped,
Give up dead beat.

Row till the sea-nymphs rise
To ask you why
Rowing you tarry not
To hear them sigh.

Row till the stars grow bright
Like certain eyes.
Row till the noon be high
As hopes you prize.

Row till you harbour in
All longing's port.
Row till you find all things
For which you sought.

T. Sturge Moore.

59. FAREWELL

N OT soon shall I forget—a sheet
　　Of golden water, cold and sweet,
The young moon with her head in veils
Of silver, and the nightingales.

A wain of hay came up the lane—
O fields I shall not walk again,
And trees I shall not see, so still
Against a sky of daffodil !

Fields where my happy heart had rest,
And where my heart was heaviest,
I shall remember them at peace
Drenched in moon-silver like a fleece.

The golden water sweet and cold,
The moon of silver and of gold,
The dew upon the gray grass-spears,
I shall remember them with tears.

Katharine Tynan.

60. A SHIP, AN ISLE, A SICKLE MOON

A ship, an isle, a sickle moon—
  With few but with how splendid stars
The mirrors of the sea are strewn
Between their silver bars !

*   *   *   *   *

An isle beside an isle she lay,
The pale ship anchored in the bay,
While in the young moon's port of gold
A star-ship—as the mirrors told—
Put forth its great and lonely light
To the unreflecting Ocean, Night.

And still, a ship upon her seas,
The isle and the island cypresses
Went sailing on without the gale :
And still there moved the moon so pale,
A crescent ship without a sail !

James Elroy Flecker.

61. NOD

SOFTLY along the road of evening,
  In a twilight dim with rose,
Wrinkled with age, and drenched with dew
  Old Nod, the shepherd, goes.

His drowsy flock streams on before him,
  Their fleeces charged with gold,
To where the sun's last beam leans low
  On Nod the shepherd's fold.

The hedge is quick and green with briar,
  From their sand the conies creep ;
And all the birds that fly in heaven
  Flock singing home to sleep.

His lambs outnumber a noon's roses,
  Yet, when night's shadows fall,
His blind old sheep-dog, Slumber-soon,
  Misses not one of all.

His are the quiet steeps of dreamland,
  The waters of no-more-pain,
His ram's bell rings 'neath an arch of stars,
  " Rest, rest, and rest again."

Walter de la Mare.

62. CHIMES

BRIEF, on a flying night,
　　From the shaken tower,
A flock of bells take flight,
　　And go with the hour.

Like birds from the cote to the gales,
　　Abrupt—O hark !
A fleet of bells set sails,
　　And go to the dark.

Sudden the cold airs swing.
　　Alone, aloud,
A verse of bells takes wing
　　And flies with the cloud.

Alice Meynell.

63. SPRING GOETH ALL IN WHITE

SPRING goeth all in white,
　　Crowned with milk-white may :
In fleecy flocks of light
O'er heaven the white clouds stray :

White butterflies in the air ;
White daisies prank the ground :
The cherry and hoary pear
Scatter their snow around.

Robert Bridges.

64. ST. VALENTINE'S DAY

To-DAY, all day, I rode upon the down,
  With hounds and horsemen, a brave company.
On this side in its glory lay the sea,
On that the Sussex weald, a sea of brown.
The wind was light, and brightly the sun shone,
And still we galloped on from gorse to gorse.
And once, when checked, a thrush sang, and my
    horse
Pricked his quick ears as to a sound unknown.
I knew the Spring was come.   I knew it even
Better than all by this, that through my chase
In bush and stone and hills and sea and heaven
I seemed to see and follow still your face.
Your face my quarry was.   For it I rode,
My horse a thing of wings, myself a god.

Wilfrid Blunt.

65. A DAY IN SUSSEX

The dove did lend me wings.   I fled away
  From the loud world which long had troubled
    me.
Oh lightly did I flee when hoyden May
Threw her wild mantle on the hawthorn-tree.
I left the dusty high-road, and my way
Was through deep meadows, shut with copses fair.
A choir of thrushes poured its roundelay
From every hedge and every thicket there.
Mild, moon-faced kine looked on, where in the grass
All heaped with flowers I lay, from noon till eve.

And hares unwitting close to me did pass,
And still the birds sang, and I could not grieve.
Oh what a blessed thing that evening was !
Peace, music, twilight, all that could deceive
A soul to joy or lull a heart to peace.
It glimmers yet across whole years like these.

Wilfrid Blunt.

66. ODE IN MAY

Let me go forth, and share
    The overflowing Sun
With one wise friend, or one
Better than wise, being fair,
Where the pewit wheels and dips
    On heights of bracken and ling,
And Earth, unto her leaflet tips,
    Tingles with the Spring.

What is so sweet and dear
    As a prosperous morn in May,
    The confident prime of the day,
And the dauntless youth of the year,
When nothing that asks for bliss,
    Asking aright, is denied,
And half of the world a bridegroom is,
    And half of the world a bride ?

The Song of Mingling flows,
    Grave, ceremonial, pure,
    As once, from lips that endure,
The cosmic descant rose,

When the temporal lord of life,
   Going his golden way,
Had taken a wondrous maid to wife
   That long had said him nay.

For of old the Sun, our sire,
   Came wooing the mother of men,
   Earth, that was virginal then,
Vestal fire to his fire.
Silent her bosom and coy,
   But the strong god sued and pressed ;
And born of their starry nuptial joy
   Are all that drink of her breast.

And the triumph of him that begot,
   And the travail of her that bore,
   Behold they are evermore
As warp and weft in our lot.
We are children of splendour and flame,
   Of shuddering, also, and tears.
Magnificent out of the dust we came,
   And abject from the Spheres.

O bright irresistible lord !
   We are fruit of Earth's womb, each one,
   And fruit of thy loins, O Sun,
Whence first was the seed outpoured.
To thee as our Father we bow,
   Forbidden thy Father to see,
Who is older and greater than thou, as thou
   Art greater and older than we.

Thou art but as a word of his speech,
   Thou art but as a wave of his hand ;
   Thou art brief as a glitter of sand
'Twixt tide and tide on his beach ;
Thou art less than a spark of his fire,
   Or a moment's mood of his soul :
Thou art lost in the notes on the lips of his choir
   That chant the chant of the Whole.

William Watson.

67. THE SCARECROW

ALL winter through I bow my head
   Beneath the driving rain ;
The North wind powders me with snow
   And blows me black again ;
At midnight 'neath a maze of stars
   I flame with glittering rime,
And stand, above the stubble, stiff
   As mail at morning-prime.
But when that child, called Spring, and all
   His host of children, come,
Scattering their buds and dew upon
   These acres of my home,
Some rapture in my rags awakes ;
   I lift void eyes and scan
The skies for crows, those ravening foes
   Of my strange master, Man.
I watch him striding lank behind
   His clashing team, and know
Soon will the wheat swish body high
   Where once lay sterile snow ;

Soon shall I gaze across a sea
  Of sun-begotten grain,
Which my unflinching watch hath sealed
  For harvest once again.

Walter de la Mare.

68. THE VAGABOND

G IVE to me the life I love,
    Let the lave go by me,
Give the jolly heaven above
  And the byway nigh me.
Bed in the bush with stars to see,
  Bread I dip in the river—
There's the life for a man like me,
  There's the life for ever.

Let the blow fall soon or late,
  Let what will be o'er me ;
Give the face of earth around
  And the road before me.
Wealth I seek not, hope nor love,
  Nor a friend to know me ;
All I seek, the heaven above
  And the road below me.

Or let autumn fall on me
  Where afield I linger,
Silencing the bird on tree,
  Biting the blue finger.
White as meal the frosty field—
  Warm the fireside haven—
Not to autumn will I yield,
  Not to winter even !

Let the blow fall soon or late,
　　Let what will be o'er me ;
Give the face of earth around
　　And the road before me.
Wealth I ask not, hope nor love,
　　Nor a friend to know me ;
All I ask, the heaven above
　　And the road below me.
　　　　　　　　　Robert Louis Stevenson.

69. TEWKESBURY ROAD

IT is good to be out on the road, and going one
　　knows not where,
　　Going through meadow and village, one knows not
　　　whither nor why ;
Through the grey light drift of the dust, in the keen
　　cool rush of the air,
　　Under the flying white clouds, and the broad blue
　　　lift of the sky.

And to halt at the chattering brook, in the tall green
　　fern at the brink
　　Where the harebell grows, and the gorse, and the
　　　foxgloves purple and white ;
Where the shy-eyed delicate deer come down in a
　　troop to drink
　　When the stars are mellow and large at the coming
　　　on of the night.

O, to feel the beat of the rain, and the homely smell
    of the earth,
  Is a tune for the blood to jig to, a joy past power
    of words ;
And the blessed green comely meadows are all a-ripple
    with mirth
  At the noise of the lambs at play and the dear wild
    cry of the birds.

John Masefield.

70. TO A LADY SEEN FROM THE TRAIN

O WHY do you walk through the fields in gloves,
  Missing so much and so much ?
O fat white woman whom nobody loves,
Why do you walk through the fields in gloves,
When the grass is soft as the breast of doves
  And shivering-sweet to the touch ?
O why do you walk through the fields in gloves,
  Missing so much and so much ?

Frances Cornford.

71. I WILL MAKE YOU BROOCHES

I WILL make you brooches and toys for your delight
  Of bird-song at morning and star-shine at night.
I will make a palace fit for you and me
Of green days in forests and blue days at sea.

I will make my kitchen, and you shall keep your
    room,
Where white flows the river and bright blows the
    broom.

And you shall wash your linen and keep your body
 white
In rainfall at morning and dewfall at night.

And this shall be for music when no one else is near,
The fine song for singing, the rare song to hear !
That only I remember, that only you admire,
Of the broad road that stretches and the roadside
 fire.

     Robert Louis Stevenson.

72. JUGGLING JERRY

Pitch here the tent, while the old horse grazes :
 By the old hedge-side we'll halt a stage.
It's nigh my last above the daisies :
 My next leaf 'll be man's blank page.
Yes, my old girl ! and it's no use crying :
 Juggler, constable, king, must bow.
One that outjuggles all 's been spying
 Long to have me, and he has me now.

We've travelled times to this old common :
 Often we've hung our pots in the gorse.
We've had a stirring life, old woman !
 You, and I, and the old grey horse.
Races, and fairs, and royal occasions,
 Found us coming to their call :
Now they'll miss us at our stations :
 There's a Juggler outjuggles all !

Up goes the lark, as if all were jolly !
   Over the duck-pond the willow shakes.
Easy to think that grieving's folly,
   When the hand's firm as driven stakes !
Ay, when we're strong, and braced, and manful,
   Life's a sweet fiddle : but we're a batch
Born to become the Great Juggler's han'ful :
   Balls he shies up, and is safe to catch.

Here's where the lads of the village cricket :
   I was a lad not wide from here :
Couldn't I whip off the bail from the wicket ?
   Like an old world those days appear !
Donkey, sheep, geese, and thatched ale-house—I
   know them !
   They are old friends of my halts, and seem,
Somehow, as if kind thanks I owe them :
   Juggling don't hinder the heart's esteem.

Juggling's no sin, for we must have victual :
   Nature allows us to bait for the fool.
Holding one's own makes us juggle no little ;
   But, to increase it, hard juggling's the rule.
You that are sneering at my profession,
   Haven't you juggled a vast amount ?
There's the Prime Minister, in one Session,
   Juggles more games than my sins'll count.

I've murdered insects with mock thunder :
   Conscience, for that, in men don't quail.
I've made bread from the bump of wonder :
   That's my business, and there's my tale.

Fashion and rank all praised the professor :
    Ay ! and I've had my smile from the Queen :
Bravo, Jerry ! she meant : God bless her !
    Ain't this a sermon on that scene ?

I've studied men from my topsy-turvy
    Close, and, I reckon, rather true.
Some are fine fellows : some, right scurvy :
    Most, a dash between the two.
But it's a woman, old girl, that makes me
    Think more kindly of the race,
And it's a woman, old girl, that shakes me
    When the Great Juggler I must face.

We two were married, due and legal :
    Honest we've lived since we've been one.
Lord ! I could then jump like an eagle :
    You danced bright as a bit o' the sun.
Birds in a May-bush we were ! right merry !
    All night we kiss'd, we juggled all day.
Joy was the heart of Juggling Jerry !
    Now from his old girl he's juggled away.

It's past parsons to console us :
    No, nor no doctor fetch for me :
I can die without my bolus ;
    Two of a trade, lass, never agree !
Parson and Doctor !—don't they love rarely,
    Fighting the devil in other men's fields !
Stand up yourself and match him fairly,
    Then see how the rascal yields !

I, lass, have lived no gipsy, flaunting
   Finery while his poor helpmate grubs :
Coin I've stored, and you won't be wanting :
   You shan't beg from the troughs and tubs.
Nobly you've stuck to me, though in his kitchen
   Many a Marquis would hail you Cook !
Palaces you could have ruled and grown rich in,
   But your old Jerry you never forsook.

Hand up the chirper ! ripe ale winks in it ;
   Let's have comfort and be at peace.
Once a stout draught made me light as a linnet.
   Cheer up ! the Lord must have his lease.
Maybe—for none see in that black hollow—
   It's just a place where we're held in pawn,
And, when the Great Juggler makes as to swallow,
   It's just the sword-trick—I ain't quite gone !

Yonder came smells of the gorse, so nutty,
   Gold-like and warm : it's the prime of May.
Better than mortar, brick and putty,
   Is God's house on a blowing day.
Lean me more up the mound ; now I feel it :
   All the old heath-smells ! Ain't it strange ?
There's the world laughing, as if to conceal it,
   But He's by us, juggling the change.

I mind it well, by the sea-beach lying,
   Once—it's long gone—when two gulls we beheld.
Which, as the moon got up, were flying
   Down a big wave that sparked and swelled.

Crack went a gun : one fell : the second
　Wheeled round him twice, and was off for new luck :
There in the dark her white wing beckon'd :—
　Drop me a kiss—I'm the bird dead-struck !

George Meredith.

73. REQUIEM

UNDER the wide and starry sky,
　Dig the grave and let me lie.
Glad did I live and gladly die,
　And I laid me down with a will.

This be the verse you grave for me :
Here he lies where he longed to be ;
Home is the sailor, home from sea,
And the hunter home from the hill.

Robert Louis Stevenson.

74. A DEAD HARVEST
In Kensington Gardens

ALONG the graceless grass of town
　They rake the rows of red and brown—
Dead leaves, unlike the rows of hay
Delicate, touched with gold and grey,
Raked long ago and far away.

A narrow silence in the park,
Between the lights a narrow dark.
One street rolls on the north ; and one,
Muffled, upon the south doth run ;
Amid the mist the work is done.

A futile crop !—for it the fire
Smoulders, and, for a stack, a pyre.
So go the town's lives on the breeze,
Even as the sheddings of the trees ;
Bosom nor barn is filled with these.

Alice Meynell.

75. THE LITTLE DANCERS

L ONELY, save for a few faint stars, the sky
   Dreams ; and lonely, below, the little street
Into its gloom retires, secluded and shy.
Scarcely the dumb roar enters this soft retreat ;
And all is dark, save where come flooding rays
From a tavern window : there, to the brisk measure
Of an organ that down in an alley merrily plays,
Two children, all alone and no one by,
Holding their tattered frocks, through an airy maze
Of motion, lightly threaded with nimble feet,
Dance sedately : face to face they gaze,
Their eyes shining, grave with a perfect pleasure.

Laurence Binyon.

76. LONDON SNOW

W HEN men were all asleep the snow came flying,
   In large white flakes falling on the city brown,
Stealthily and perpetually settling and loosely lying,
   Hushing the latest traffic of the drowsy town ;
Deadening, muffling, stifling its murmurs failing ;
Lazily and incessantly floating down and down :
   Silently sifting and veiling road, roof and railing ;

Hiding difference, making unevenness even,
Into angles and crevices softly drifting and sailing.
  All night it fell, and when full inches seven
It lay in the depth of its uncompacted lightness,
The clouds blew off from a high and frosty heaven ;
  And all woke earlier for the unaccustomed bright-
    ness
Of the winter dawning, the strange unheavenly glare :
The eye marvelled—marvelled at the dazzling white-
    ness ;
  The ear hearkened to the stillness of the solemn air ;
No sound of wheel rumbling nor of foot falling,
And the busy morning cries came thin and spare.
  Then boys I heard, as they went to school, calling,
They gathered up the crystal manna to freeze
Their tongues with tasting, their hands with snow-
    balling ;
  Or rioted in a drift, plunging up to the knees ;
Or peering up from under the white-mossed wonder,
" O look at the trees ! " they cried, " O look at the
    trees ! "
  With lessened load a few carts creak and blunder,
Following along the white deserted way,
A country company long dispersed asunder :
  When now already the sun, in pale display
Standing by Paul's high dome, spread forth below
His sparkling beams, and awoke the stir of the day.
  For now doors open, and war is waged with the
    snow ;
And trains of sombre men, past tale of number,
Tread long brown paths, as toward their toil they go ;

But even for them awhile no cares encumber
Their minds diverted ; the daily word is unspoken,
The daily thoughts of labour and sorrow slumber
At the sight of the beauty that greets them, for the
    charm they have broken.

Robert Bridges.

77. THE ROAD MENDERS

How solitary gleams the lamplit street
    Waiting the far-off morn !
How softly from the unresting city blows
    The murmur borne
    Down this deserted way !
Dim loiterers pass home with stealthy feet.
Now only, sudden at their interval,
The lofty chimes awaken and let fall
    Deep thrills of ordered sound ;
Subsiding echoes gradually drowned
In a great stillness, that creeps up around,
    And darkly grows
    Profounder over all
Like a strong frost, hushing a stormy day.

But who is this, that by the brazier red
    Encamped in his rude hut,
With many a sack about his shoulder spread
    Watches with eyes unshut ?
The burning brazier flushes his old face,
Illumining the old thoughts in his eyes.
Surely the Night doth to her secrecies
Admit him, and the watching stars attune

To their high patience, who so lightly seems
To bear the weight of many thousand dreams
(Dark hosts around him sleeping numberless) ;
He surely hath unbuilt all walls of thought
To reach an air-wide wisdom, past access
Of us, who labour in the noisy noon,
The noon that knows him not.

For lo, at last the gloom slowly retreats,
And swiftly, like an army, comes the Day,
All bright and loud through the awakened streets
Sending a cheerful hum.
And he has stolen away.
Now, with the morning shining round them, come
Young men, and strip their coats
And loose the shirts about their throats,
And lightly up their ponderous hammers lift,
Each in his turn descending swift
With triple strokes that answer and begin
Duly, and quiver in repeated change,
Marrying the eager echoes that weave in
A music clear and strange.
But pausing soon, each lays his hammer down
And deeply breathing bares
His chest, stalwart and brown,
To the sunny airs.
Laughing one to another, limber hand
On limber hip, flushed in a group they stand,
And now untired renew their ringing toil.
The sun stands high, and ever a fresh throng
Comes murmuring ; but that eddying turmoil

Leaves many a loiterer, prosperous or unfed,
On easy or unhappy ways
At idle gaze,
Charmed in the sunshine and the rhythm enthralling,
As of unwearied Fates, for ever young,
That on the anvil of necessity
From measureless desire and quivering fear,
With musical sure lifting and downfalling
Of arm and hammer driven perpetually,
Beat out in obscure span
The fiery destiny of man.

Laurence Binyon.

78. STREET LANTERNS

COUNTRY roads are yellow and brown.
We mend the roads in London town.

Never a hansom dare come nigh,
Never a cart goes rolling by.

An unwonted silence steals
In between the turning wheels.

Quickly ends the autumn day,
And the workman goes his way,

Leaving, midst the traffic rude,
One small isle of solitude,

Lit, throughout the lengthy night,
By the little lantern's light.

Jewels of the dark have we,
Brighter than the rustic's be.

Over the dull earth are thrown
Topaz, and the ruby stone.

Mary E. Coleridge.

79. O SUMMER SUN

O SUMMER sun, O moving trees !
      O cheerful human noise, O busy glittering
   street !
What hour shall Fate in all the future find,
Or what delights, ever to equal these :
Only to taste the warmth, the light, the wind,
Only to be alive, and feel that life is sweet ?

Laurence Binyon.

80. LONDON

A THWART the sky a lowly sigh
      From west to east the sweet wind carried ;
The sun stood still on Primrose Hill ;
   His light in all the city tarried :
The clouds on viewless columns bloomed
Like smouldering lilies unconsumed.

" Oh sweetheart, see ! how shadowy,
   Of some occult magician's rearing,
Or swung in space of heaven's grace
   Dissolving, dimly reappearing,
Afloat upon ethereal tides
St. Paul's above the city rides ! "

A rumour broke through the thin smoke
  Enwreathing abbey, tower, and palace,
The parks, the squares, the thoroughfares,
  The million-peopled lanes and alleys,
An ever-muttering prisoned storm,
The heart of London beating warm.

John Davidson.

81. NOVEMBER BLUE

The golden tint of the electric lights seems to give a comple-
mentary colour to the air in the early evening.—*Essay on London.*

O HEAVENLY colour, London town
    Has blurred it from her skies ;
And, hooded in an earthly brown,
    Unheaven'd the city lies.
No longer standard-like this hue
    Above the broad road flies ;
Nor does the narrow street the blue
    Wear, slender pennon-wise.

But when the gold and silver lamps
    Colour the London dew,
And, misted by the winter damps,
    The shops shine bright anew—
Blue comes to earth, it walks the street,
    It dyes the wide air through ;
A mimic sky about their feet,
    The throng go crowned with blue.

Alice Meynell.

P.T.D. I—4

82. PHILOMEL IN LONDON

NOT within a granite pass,
  Dim with flowers and soft with grass—
Nay, but doubly, trebly sweet
In a poplared London street,
While below my windows go
Noiseless barges, to and fro,
    Through the night's calm deep,
Ah ! what breaks the bonds of sleep ?

No steps on the pavement fall,
Soundless swings the dark canal ;
From a church-tower out of sight
Clangs the central hour of night.
Hark ! the Dorian nightingale !
Pan's voice melted to a wail !
    Such another bird
Attic Tereus never heard.

Hung above the gloom and stain—
London's squalid cope of pain—
Pure as starlight, bold as love,
Honouring our scant poplar-grove,
That most heavenly voice of earth
Thrills in passion, grief or mirth,
    Laves our poison'd air
Life's best song-bath crystal-fair.

While the starry minstrel sings
Little matters what he brings,
Be it sorrow, be it pain,
Let him sing and sing again,

Till, with dawn, poor souls rejoice,
Wakening, once to hear his voice,
   Ere afar he flies,
Bound for purer woods and skies.

                 Edmund Gosse.

83. ANNUS MIRABILIS (1902)

DAYLIGHT was down, and up the cool
   Bare heaven the moon, o'er roof and elm,
Daughter of dusk most wonderful,
   Went mounting to her realm :
And night was only half begun
Round Edwardes Square in Kensington.

A Sabbath-calm possessed her face,
   An even glow her bosom filled ;
High in her solitary place
   The huntress-heart was stilled :
With bow and arrows all laid down
She stood and looked on London town.

Nay, how can sight of us give rest
   To that far-travelled heart, or draw
The musings of that tranquil breast ?
   I thought—and gazing, saw
Far up above me, high, oh, high,
From south to north a heron fly !

Oh, swiftly answered ! yonder flew
   The wings of freedom and of hope !
Little of London town he knew,
   The far horizon was his scope.

High up he sails, and sees beneath
The glimmering ponds of Hampstead Heath,

Hendon, and farther out afield
    Low water-meads are in his ken,
And lonely pools by Harrow Weald,
    And solitudes unloved of men,
Where he his fisher's spear dips down :
Little he knows of London town.

So small, with all its miles of sin,
    Is London to the grey-winged bird,
A cuckoo called at Lincoln's Inn
    Last April ; in Soho was heard
The missel-thrush with throat of glee,
And nightingales at Battersea !

Laurence Housman.

84. FLEET STREET

I NEVER see the newsboys run
    Amid the whirling street,
    With swift untiring feet,
To cry the latest venture done,
But I expect one day to hear
    Them cry the crack of doom
    And risings from the tomb,
With great Archangel Michael near ;
And see them running from the Fleet
    As messengers of God,
    With Heaven's tidings shod
About their brave unwearied feet.

Shane Leslie.

85. IN THE MEADOWS AT MANTUA

BUT to have lain upon the grass
    One perfect day, one perfect hour,
Beholding all things mortal pass
Into the quiet of green grass ;

But to have lain and loved the sun,
Under the shadow of the trees,
To have been found in unison,
Once only, with the blessed sun ;

Ah ! in these flaring London nights,
Where midnight withers into morn,
How quiet a rebuke it writes
Across the sky of London nights !

Upon the grass at Mantua
These London nights were all forgot.
They wake for me again : but ah,
The meadow-grass at Mantua !

Arthur Symons.

86. LEISURE

WHAT is this life if, full of care,
    We have no time to stand and stare.

No time to stand beneath the boughs
And stare as long as sheep or cows.

No time to see, when woods we pass,
Where squirrels hide their nuts in grass.

No time to see, in broad daylight,
Streams full of stars, like skies at night.

No time to turn at Beauty's glance,
And watch her feet, how they can dance.

No time to wait till her mouth can
Enrich that smile her eyes began.

A poor life this if, full of care,
We have no time to stand and stare.
William H. Davies.

87. LYING IN THE GRASS

BETWEEN two russet tufts of summer grass,
    I watch the world through hot air as through
        glass,
And by my face sweet lights and colours pass.

Before me, dark against the fading sky,
I watch three mowers mowing, as I lie :
With brawny arms they sweep in harmony.

Brown English faces by the sun burnt red,
Rich glowing colour on bare throat and head,
My heart would leap to watch them, were I dead !

And in my strong young living as I lie,
I seem to move with them in harmony,—
A fourth is mowing, and that fourth am I.

The music of the scythes that glide and leap,
The young men whistling as their great arms sweep,
And all the perfume and sweet sense of sleep,

The weary butterflies that droop their wings,
The dreamy nightingale that hardly sings,
And all the lassitude of happy things

Is mingling with the warm and pulsing blood
That gushes through my veins a languid flood,
And feeds my spirit as the sap a bud.

Behind the mowers, on the amber air,
A dark-green beech-wood rises, still and fair,
A white path winding up it like a stair.

And see that girl, with pitcher on her head,
And clean white apron on her gown of red,—
Her even-song of love is but half-said :

She waits the youngest mower. Now he goes ;
Her cheeks are redder than the wild blush-rose ;
They climb up where the deepest shadows close.

But though they pass and vanish, I am there ;
I watch his rough hands meet beneath her hair,
Their broken speech sounds sweet to me like prayer.

Ah ! now the rosy children come to play,
And romp and struggle with the new-mown hay ;
Their clear high voices sound from far away.

They know so little why the world is sad,
They dig themselves warm graves and yet are glad ;
Their muffled screams and laughter make me mad !

I long to go and play among them there,
Unseen, like wind, to take them by the hair,
And gently make their rosy cheeks more fair.

The happy children ! full of frank surprise,
And sudden whims and innocent ecstasies ;
What godhead sparkles from their liquid eyes !

No wonder round those urns of mingled clays
That Tuscan potters fashion'd in old days,
And coloured like the torrid earth ablaze,

We find the little gods and loves portray'd
Through ancient forests wandering undismay'd,
Or gathered, whispering, in some pleasant glade.

They knew, as I do now, what keen delight
A strong man feels to watch the tender flight
Of little children playing in his sight.

I do not hunger for a well-stored mind,
I only wish to live my life, and find
My heart in unison with all mankind.

My life is like the single dewy star
That trembles on the horizon's primrose-bar,—
A microcosm where all things living are.

And if, among the noiseless grasses, Death
Should come behind and take away my breath,
I should not rise as one who sorroweth ;

For I should pass, but all the world would be
Full of desire and young delight and glee,
And why should men be sad through loss of me ?

The light is dying ; in the silver-blue
The young moon shines from her bright window
    through :
The mowers all are gone, and I go too.

Edmund Gosse.

88. DOWN BY THE SALLEY GARDENS

DOWN by the salley gardens my love and I did
    meet ;
She passed the salley gardens with little snow-white
    feet.
She bid me take love easy, as the leaves grow on the
    tree ;
But I, being young and foolish, with her would not
    agree.

In a field by the river my love and I did stand,
And on my leaning shoulder she laid her snow-white
    hand.
She bid me take life easy, as the grass grows on the
    weirs ;
But I was young and foolish, and now am full of tears.

P.T.D. I—4*

W. B. Yeats.

89. RENAISSANCE

O HAPPY soul, forget thy self !
    This that has haunted all the past,
That conjured disappointments fast,
That never could let well alone ;
That, climbing to achievement's throne,
Slipped on the last step ; this that wove
Dissatisfaction's clinging net,
And ran through life like squandered pelf :—
This that till now has been thy self
Forget, O happy soul, forget.

If ever thou didst aught commence,—
Set'st forth in springtide woods to rove,—
Or, when the sun in July throve,
Didst plunge into calm bay of ocean
With fine felicity in motion,—
Or, having climbed some high hill's brow,
Thy toil behind thee like the night,
Stoodst in the chill dawn's air intense ;—
Commence thus now, thus recommence :
Take to the future as to light.

Not as a bather on the shore
Strips off his clothes, glad soul, strip thou :
He throws them off, but folds them now ;
Although he for the billows yearns,
To weight them down with stones he turns ;
To mark the spot he scans the shore ;
Of his return he thinks before.
Do thou forget

All that, until this joy franchised thee,
Tainted thee, stained thee, or disguised thee ;
For gladness, henceforth without let,
Be thou a body, naked, fair ;
And be thy kingdom all the air
Which the noon fills with light ;
And be thine actions every one,
Like to a dawn or set of sun,
Robed in an ample glory's peace ;
Since thou hast tasted this great glee
Whose virtue prophesies in thee
That wrong is wholly doomed, is doomed and bound
    to cease.

T. Sturge Moore.

90. TO WILL. H. LOW

YOUTH now flees on feathered foot
    Faint and fainter sounds the flute,
Rarer songs of gods ; and still
Somewhere on the sunny hill,
Or along the winding stream,
Through the willows, flits a dream ;
Flits but shows a smiling face,
Flees but with so quaint a grace,
None can choose to stay at home,
All must follow, all must roam.

This is unborn beauty : she
Now in air floats high and free,
Takes the sun and breaks the blue ;—
Late with stooping pinion flew

Raking hedgerow trees, and wet
Her wing in silver streams, and set
Shining foot on temple roof :
Now again she flies aloof,
Coasting mountain clouds and kiss't
By the evening's amethyst.

In wet wood and miry lane,
Still we pant and pound in vain ;
Still with leaden foot we chase
Waning pinion, fainting face ;
Still with gray hair we stumble on,
Till, behold, the vision gone !
Where hath fleeting beauty led ?
To the doorway of the dead.
Life is over, life was gay :
We have come the primrose way.

Robert Louis Stevenson.

91. GAUDEAMUS IGITUR

COME, no more of grief and dying !
    Sing the time too swiftly flying.
        Just an hour
        Youth's in flower,
Give me roses to remember
In the shadow of December.

Fie on steeds with leaden paces !
Winds shall bear us on our races,
        Speed, O speed,
        Wind, my steed,
Beat the lightning for your master,
Yet my Fancy shall fly faster.

Give me music, give me rapture,
Youth that's fled can none recapture;
    Not with thought
    Wisdom's bought.
Out on pride and scorn and sadness!
Give me laughter, give me gladness.

Sweetest Earth, I love and love thee,
Seas about thee, skies above thee,
    Sun and storms,
    Hues and forms
Of the clouds with floating shadows
On thy mountains and thy meadows.

Earth, there's none that can enslave thee,
Not thy lords it is that have thee;
    Not for gold
    Art thou sold,
But thy lovers at their pleasure
Take thy beauty and thy treasure.

While sweet fancies meet me singing,
While the April blood is springing
    In my breast,
    While a jest
And my youth thou yet must leave me,
Fortune, 'tis not thou canst grieve me.

When at length the grasses cover
Me, the world's unwearied lover,
    If regret
    Haunt me yet,

It shall be for joys untasted,
Nature lent and folly wasted.

Youth and jests and summer weather,
Goods that kings and clowns together
      Waste or use
      As they choose,
These, the best, we miss pursuing
Sullen shades that mock our wooing.

Feigning Age will not delay it—
When the reckoning comes we'll pay it,
      Own our mirth
      Has been worth
All the forfeit light or heavy
Wintry Time and Fortune levy.

Feigning grief will not escape it,
What though ne'er so well you ape it—
      Age and care
      All must share,
All alike must pay hereafter,
Some for sighs and some for laughter.

Know, ye sons of Melancholy,
To be young and wise is folly.
      'Tis the weak
      Fear to wreak
On this clay of life their fancies,
Shaping battles, shaping dances.

While ye scorn our names unspoken,
Roses dead and garlands broken,
    O ye wise,
    We arise,
Out of failures, dreams, disasters,
We arise to be your masters.
Margaret L. Woods.

92. O DREAMY, GLOOMY, FRIENDLY TREES!

O DREAMY, gloomy, friendly Trees,
    I came along your narrow track
To bring my gifts unto your knees
    And gifts did you give back;
For when I brought this heart that burns—
    These thoughts that bitterly repine—
And laid them here among the ferns
    And the hum of boughs divine,
Ye, vastest breathers of the air,
    Shook down with slow and mighty poise
Your coolness on the human care,
    Your wonder on its toys,
Your greenness on the heart's despair,
    Your darkness on its noise.
Herbert Trench.

93. IDLENESS

O IDLENESS, too fond of me,
    Begone, I know and hate thee!
Nothing canst thou of pleasure see
    In one that so doth rate thee;

For empty are both mind and heart
　　While thou with me dost linger;
More profit would to thee impart
　　A babe that sucks its finger.

I know thou hast a better way
　　To spend these hours thou squand'rest;
Some lad toils in the trough to-day
　　Who groans because thou wand'rest;

A bleating sheep he dowses now
　　Or wrestles with ram's terror;
Ah, 'mid the washing's hubbub, how
　　His sighs reproach thine error!

He knows and loves thee, Idleness;
　　For when his sheep are browsing,
His open eyes enchant and bless
　　A mind divinely drowsing;

No slave to sleep, he wills and sees
　　From hill-lawns the brown tillage;
Green winding lanes and clumps of trees,
　　Far town or nearer village,

The sea itself; the fishing fleet
　　Where more, thine idle lovers,
Heark'ning to sea-mews find thee sweet
　　Like him who hears the plovers.

Begone; those haul their ropes at sea,
　　These plunge sheep in yon river:
Free, free from toil thy friends, and me
　　From Idleness deliver!

T. Sturge Moore.

94. YOUTH AND LOVE

To the heart of youth the world is a highwayside.
  Passing for ever, he fares ; and on either hand,
Deep in the gardens golden pavilions hide,
Nestle in orchard bloom, and far on the level land
Call him with lighted lamp in the eventide.

Thick as the stars at night when the moon is down,
Pleasures assail him.   He to his nobler fate
Fares ; and but waves a hand as he passes on,
Cries but a wayside word to her at the garden gate,
Sings but a boyish stave and his face is gone.

Robert Louis Stevenson.

95. THE PRECEPT OF SILENCE

I know you : solitary griefs,
  Desolate passions, aching hours !
I know you : tremulous beliefs,
Agonised hopes, and ashen flowers !

The winds are sometimes sad to me ;
The starry spaces, full of fear :
Mine is the sorrow on the sea,
And mine the sigh of places drear.

Some players upon plaintive strings
Publish their wistfulness abroad :
I have not spoken of these things,
Save to one man, and unto God.

Lionel Johnson.

96. IF THIS WERE FAITH

GOD, if this were enough,
    That I see things bare to the buff
And up to the buttocks in mire ;
That I ask nor hope nor hire,
Nut in the husk,
Nor dawn beyond the dusk,
Nor life beyond death :
God, if this were faith ?

Having felt thy wind in my face
Spit sorrow and disgrace,
Having seen thine evil doom
In Golgotha and Khartoum,
And the brutes, the work of thine hands,
Fill with injustice lands
And stain with blood the sea :
If still in my veins the glee
Of the black night and the sun
And the lost battle, run :
If, an adept,
The iniquitous lists I still accept
With joy, and joy to endure and be withstood,
And still to battle and perish for a dream of good :
God, if that were enough ?

If to feel, in the ink of the slough,
And the sink of the mire,
Veins of glory and fire
Run through and transpierce and transpire,
And a secret purpose of glory in every part,

And the answering glory of battle fill my heart ;
To thrill with the joy of girded men,
To go on for ever and fail and go on again,
And be mauled to the earth and arise,
And contend for the shade of a word and a thing not
    seen with the eyes :
With the half of a broken hope for a pillow at night
That somehow the right is the right
And the smooth shall bloom from the rough :
Lord, if that were enough ?

Robert Louis Stevenson.

97. VITAI LAMPADA

THERE'S a breathless hush in the Close to night—
    Ten to make and the match to win—
A bumping pitch and a blinding light,
    An hour to play and the last man in.
And it's not for the sake of a ribboned coat,
    Or the selfish hope of a season's fame,
But his Captain's hand on his shoulder smote :
    " Play up ! play up ! and play the game ! "

The sand of the desert is sodden red,—
    Red with the wreck of a square that broke ;—
The Gatling's jammed and the Colonel dead,
    And the regiment blind with dust and smoke.
The river of death has brimmed his banks,
    And England's far, and Honour a name,
But the voice of a schoolboy rallies the ranks :
    " Play up ! play up ! and play the game ! "

This is the word that year by year,
    While in her place the School is set,
Every one of her sons must hear,
    And none that hears it dare forget.
This they all with a joyful mind
    Bear through life like a torch in flame,
And falling fling to the host behind—
    " Play up ! play up ! and play the game ! "

Henry Newbolt.

98. LAUGH AND BE MERRY

LAUGH and be merry, remember, better the world
    with a song,
Better the world with a blow in the teeth of a wrong.
Laugh, for the time is brief, a thread the length of a
    span.
Laugh, and be proud to belong to the old proud
    pageant of man.

Laugh and be merry : remember, in olden time,
God made Heaven and Earth for joy He took in a
    rhyme,
Made them, and filled them full with the strong red
    wine of His mirth,
The splendid joy of the stars : the joy of the earth.

So we must laugh and drink from the deep blue cup
    of the sky,
Join the jubilant song of the great stars sweeping by,
Laugh, and battle, and work, and drink of the wine
    outpoured
In the dear green earth, the sign of the joy of the
    Lord.

Laugh and be merry together, like brothers akin,
Guesting awhile in the rooms of a beautiful inn,
Glad till the dancing stops, and the lilt of the music
ends.
Laugh till the game is played ; and be you merry,
my friends.

John Masefield.

99. ROUNDABOUTS AND SWINGS

IT was early last September nigh to Framlin'am-
on Sea,
An' 'twas Fair-day come to-morrow, an' the time
was after tea,
An' I met a painted caravan adown a dusty lane,
A Pharaoh with his waggons comin' jolt an' creak an'
strain ;
A cheery cove an' sunburnt, bold o' eye and wrinkled
up,
An' beside him on the splashboard sat a brindled
tarrier pup,
An' a lurcher wise as Solomon an' lean as fiddle-
strings
Was joggin' in the dust along 'is roundabouts and
swings.

" Goo'-day," said 'e ; " Goo'-day," said I ; " an'
'ow d'you find things go,
An' what's the chance o' millions when you runs a
travellin' show ? "

" I find," said 'e, " things very much as 'ow I've
    always found,
For mostly they goes up and down or else goes round
    and round."
Said 'e, " The job's the very spit o' what it always
    were,
It's bread and bacon mostly when the dog don't
    catch a 'are ;
But lookin' at it broad, an' while it ain't no merchant
    king's,
What's lost upon the roundabouts we pulls up on
    the swings ! "

" Goo' luck," said 'e ; " Goo' luck," said I ; " you've
    put it past a doubt ;
An' keep that lurcher on the road, the gamekeepers
    is out " ;
'E thumped upon the footboard an' 'e lumbered on
    again
To meet a gold-dust sunset down the owl-light in
    the lane ;
An' the moon she climbed the 'azels, while a nightjar
    seemed to spin
That Pharaoh's wisdom o'er again, 'is sooth of lose-
    and-win ;
For " up an' down an' round," said 'e, " goes all
    appointed things,
An' losses on the roundabouts means profits on the
    swings ! "

Patrick R. Chalmers.

100. THE LARK ASCENDING

HE rises and begins to round,
He drops the silver chain of sound,
Of many links without a break,
In chirrup, whistle, slur and shake,
All intervolved and spreading wide,
Like water-dimples down a tide
Where ripple ripple overcurls
And eddy into eddy whirls ;
A press of hurried notes that run
So fleet they scarce are more than one,
Yet changeingly the trills repeat
And linger ringing while they fleet,
Sweet to the quick o' the ear, and dear
To her beyond the handmaid ear,
Who sits beside our inner springs,
Too often dry for this he brings,
Which seems the very jet of earth
At sight of sun, her music's mirth,
As up he wings the spiral stair,
A song of light, and pierces air
With fountain ardour, fountain play,
To reach the shining tops of day,
And drink in everything discerned
An ecstasy to music turned,
Impelled by what his happy bill
Disperses ; drinking, showering still,
Unthinking save that he may give
His voice the outlet, there to live
Renewed in endless notes of glee,
So thirsty of his voice is he,

For all to hear and all to know
That he is joy, awake, aglow,
The tumult of the heart to hear
Through pureness filtered crystal-clear,
And know the pleasure sprinkled bright
By simple singing of delight,
Shrill, irreflective, unrestrained,
Rapt, ringing, on the jet sustained
Without a break, without a fall,
Sweet-silvery, sheer lyrical,
Perennial, quavering up the chord
Like myriad dews of sunny sward
That trembling into fulness shine,
And sparkle dropping argentine ;
Such wooing as the ear receives
From zephyr caught in choric leaves
Of aspens when their chattering net
Is flushed to white with shivers wet ;
And such the water-spirit's chime
On mountain heights in morning's prime,
Too freshly sweet to seem excess,
Too animate to need a stress ;
But wider over many heads
The starry voice ascending spreads,
Awakening, as it waxes thin,
The best in us to him akin ;
And every face, to watch him raised,
Puts on the light of children praised,
So rich our human pleasure ripes
When sweetness on sincereness pipes,
Though nought be promised from the seas,

But only a soft-ruffling breeze
Sweep glittering on a still content,
Serenity in ravishment.

For singing till his heaven fills,
'Tis love of earth that he instils,
And ever winging up and up,
Our valley is his golden cup,
And he the wine which overflows
To lift us with him as he goes :
The woods and brooks, the sheep and kine,
He is, the hills, the human line,
The meadows green, the fallows brown,
The dreams of labour in the town ;
He sings the sap, the quickened veins ;
The wedding song of sun and rains
He is, the dance of children, thanks
Of sowers, shout of primrose-banks,
And eye of violets while they breathe ;
All these the circling song will wreathe,
And you shall hear the herb and tree,
The better heart of men shall see,
Shall feel celestially, as long
As you crave nothing save the song.

Was never voice of ours could say
Our inmost in the sweetest way,
Like yonder voice aloft, and link
All hearers in the song they drink.
Our wisdom speaks from failing blood,
Our passion is too full in flood,

We want the key of his wild note
Of truthful in a tuneful throat,
The song seraphically free
Of taint of personality,
So pure that it salutes the suns
The voice of one for millions,
In whom the millions rejoice
For giving their one spirit voice.

Yet men have we, whom we revere,
Now names, and men still housing here,
Whose lives, by many a battle-dint
Defaced, and grinding wheels on flint,
Yield substance, though they sing not, sweet
For song our highest heaven to greet:
Whom heavenly singing gives us new,
Enspheres them brilliant in our blue,
From firmest base to farthest leap,
Because their love of Earth is deep,
And they are warriors in accord
With life to serve, and pass reward,
So touching purest and so heard
In the brain's reflex of yon bird:
Wherefore their soul in me or mine,
Through self-forgetfulness divine,
In them, that song aloft maintains,
To fill the sky and thrill the plains
With showerings drawn from human stores,
As he to silence nearer soars,
Extends the world at wings and dome,
More spacious making more our home,

Till lost on his aerial rings
In light, and then the fancy sings.
George Meredith.

101. INTO THE TWILIGHT

OUT-WORN heart, in a time out-worn,
    Come clear of the nets of wrong and right ;
Laugh, heart, again in the gray twilight ;
Sigh, heart, again in the dew of the morn.

Your mother Eire is always young,
Dew ever shining and twilight gray ;
Though hope fall from you and love decay
Burning in fires of a slanderous tongue.

Come, heart, where hill is heaped upon hill ;
For there the mystical brotherhood
Of sun and moon and hollow and wood
And river and stream work out their will ;

And God stands winding His lonely horn ;
And time and the world are ever in flight,
And love is less kind than the gray twilight,
And hope is less dear than the dew of the morn.
W. B. Yeats.

102. BY A BIER-SIDE

THIS is a sacred city built of marvellous earth.
    Life was lived nobly here to give such beauty
birth.

Beauty was in this brain and in this eager hand :
Death is so blind and dumb Death does not under-
    stand.
Death drifts the brain with dust and soils the young
    limbs' glory,
Death makes justice a dream, and strength a traveller's
    story.
Death drives the lovely soul to wander under the sky.
Death opens unknown doors. It is most grand to die.

John Masefield.

103. 'TIS BUT A WEEK

'TIS but a week since down the glen
    The trampling horses came
—Half a hundred fighting men
    With all their spears aflame !
They laughed and clattered as they went,
    And round about their way
The blackbirds sang with one consent
    In the green leaves of May.

Never again shall I see them pass ;
    They'll come victorious never ;
Their spears are withered all as grass,
    Their laughter's laid for ever ;
And where they clattered as they went,
    And where their hearts were gay,
The blackbirds sing with one consent
    In the green leaves of May.

Gerald Gould.

104. I LOVE ALL BEAUTEOUS THINGS

I LOVE all beauteous things,
  I seek and adore them;
God hath no better praise,
And man in his hasty days
  Is honoured for them.

I too will something make
  And joy in the making;
Altho' to-morrow it seem
Like the empty words of a dream
  Remembered on waking.
                    Robert Bridges.

105. ALL FLESH

I DO not need the skies'
  Pomp, when I would be wise;
For pleasaunce nor to use
Heaven's champaign when I muse.
One grass-blade in its veins
Wisdom's whole flood contains:
Thereon my foundering mind
Odyssean fate can find.

O little blade, now vaunt
Thee, and be arrogant!
Tell the proud sun that he
Sweated in shaping thee;
Night, that she did unvest
Her mooned and argent breast
To suckle thee.   Heaven fain

Yearned over thee in rain,
And with wide parent wing
Shadowed thee, nested thing,
Fed thee, and slaved for thy
Impotent tyranny.
Nature's broad thews bent
Meek for thy content.
Mastering littleness
Which the wise heavens confess,
The frailty which doth draw
Magnipotence to its law—
These were, O happy one, these
Thy laughing puissances !

Be confident of thought,
Seeing that thou art naught ;
And be thy pride thou'rt all
Delectably safe and small.
Epitomized in thee
Was the mystery
Which shakes the spheres conjoint—
God focussed to a point.

All thy fine mouths shout
Scorn upon dull-eyed doubt.
Impenetrable fool
Is he thou canst not school
To the humility
By which the angels see !
Unfathomably framed
Sister, I am not shamed

Before the cherubin
To vaunt my flesh thy kin.
My one hand thine, and one
Imprisoned in God's own,
I am as God ; alas,
And such a god of grass !
A little root clay-caught,
A wind, a flame, a thought,
Inestimably naught !

                        Francis Thompson.

106. TO A SNOWFLAKE

WHAT heart could have thought you ?—
            Past our devisal
(O filigree petal !)
Fashioned so purely,
Fragilely, surely,
From what Paradisal
Imagineless metal,
Too costly for cost ?
Who hammered you, wrought you,
From argentine vapour ?—
" God was my shaper.
Passing surmisal,
He hammered, He wrought me,
From curled silver vapour,
To lust of His mind :—
Thou couldst not have thought me !
So purely, so palely,
Tinily, surely,
Mightily, frailly,

Insculped and embossed,
With His hammer of wind,
And His graver of frost."

Francis Thompson.

107. TO A DAISY

SLIGHT as thou art, thou art enough to hide,
   Like all created things, secrets from me,
And stand a barrier to eternity.
And I, how can I praise thee well and wide

From where I dwell—upon the hither side ?
   Thou little veil for so great mystery,
   When shall I penetrate all things and thee,
And then look back ?   For this I must abide,

Till thou shalt grow and fold and be unfurled
Literally between me and the world.
   Then I shall drink from in beneath a spring,

And from a poet's side shall read his book.
O daisy mine, what will it be to look
   From God's side even of such a simple thing ?

Alice Meynell.

108. LUCIFER IN STARLIGHT

ON a starred night Prince Lucifer uprose.
   Tired of his dark dominion swung the fiend
Above the rolling ball in cloud part screened,
Where sinners hugged their spectre of repose.

Poor prey to his hot fit of pride were those.
And now upon his western wing he leaned,
Now his huge bulk o'er Afric's sands careened,
Now the black planet shadowed Arctic snows.
Soaring through wider zones that pricked his scars
With memory of the old revolt from Awe,
He reached a middle height, and at the stars,
Which are the brain of heaven, he looked, and sank.
Around the ancient track marched rank on rank,
The army of unalterable law.

George Meredith.

109. THE CELESTIAL SURGEON

IF I have faltered more or less
In my great task of happiness ;
If I have moved among my race
And shown no glorious morning face ;
If beams from happy human eyes
Have moved me not ; if morning skies,
Books, and my food, and summer rain
Knocked on my sullen heart in vain :—
Lord, thy most pointed pleasure take
And stab my spirit broad awake ;
Or, Lord, if too obdurate I,
Choose thou, before that spirit die,
A piercing pain, a killing sin,
And to my dead heart run them in !

Robert Louis Stevenson.

110. THE KINGDOM OF GOD
'In no Strange Land'

O WORLD invisible, we view thee,
   O world intangible, we touch thee,
O world unknowable, we know thee,
   Inapprehensible, we clutch thee !

Does the fish soar to find the ocean,
   The eagle plunge to find the air—
That we ask of the stars in motion
   If they have rumour of thee there ?

Not where the wheeling systems darken,
   And our benumbed conceiving soars !—
The drift of pinions, would we hearken,
   Beats at our own clay-shuttered doors.

The angels keep their ancient places ;—
   Turn but a stone, and start a wing !
'Tis ye, 'tis your estrangèd faces,
   That miss the many-splendoured thing.

But (when so sad thou canst not sadder)
   Cry ;—and upon thy so sore loss
Shall shine the traffic of Jacob's ladder
   Pitched betwixt Heaven and Charing Cross.

Yea, in the night, my Soul, my daughter,
   Cry,—clinging Heaven by the hems ;
And lo, Christ walking on the water
   Not of Gennesareth, but Thames !

Francis Thompson.

111. THE LADY POVERTY

THE Lady Poverty was fair :
    But she has lost her looks of late,
With change of times and change of air.
Ah slattern ! she neglects her hair,
Her gown, her shoes ; she keeps no state
As once when her pure feet were bare.

Or—almost worse, if worse can be—
She scolds in parlours, dusts and trims,
Watches and counts.   Oh, is this she
Whom Francis met, whose step was free,
Who with Obedience carolled hymns,
In Umbria walked with Chastity ?

Where is her ladyhood ?   Not here,
Not among modern kinds of men ;
But in the stony fields, where clear
Through the thin trees the skies appear,
In delicate spare soil and fen,
And slender landscape and austere.

                              Alice Meynell.

112. COURTESY

OF Courtesy it is much less
    Than Courage of Heart or Holiness
Yet in my Walks it seems to me
That the Grace of God is in Courtesy.

On Monks I did in Storrington fall,
They took me straight into their Hall ;
I saw Three Pictures on a wall,
And Courtesy was in them all.

The first the Annunciation ;
The second the Visitation ;
The third the Consolation,
Of God that was Our Lady's Son.

The first was of Saint Gabriel ;
On Wings a-flame from Heaven he fell ;
And as he went upon one knee
He shone with Heavenly Courtesy.

Our Lady out of Nazareth rode—
It was her month of heavy load ;
Yet was Her face both great and kind,
For Courtesy was in Her Mind.

The third, it was our Little Lord,
Whom all the Kings in arms adored ;
He was so small you could not see
His large intent of Courtesy.

Our Lord, that was Our Lady's Son,
Go bless you, People, one by one ;
My Rhyme is written, my work is done.

Hilaire Belloc.

113. MONTSERRAT

PEACE waits among the hills ;
    I have drunk peace,
Here, where the blue air fills
The great cup of the hills,
And fills with peace.

Between the earth and sky,
I have seen the earth
Like a dark cloud go by,
And fade out of the sky ;
There was no more earth.

Here, where the Holy Graal
Brought secret light
Once, from beyond the veil,
I, seeing no Holy Graal,
See divine light.

Light fills the hills with God,
Wind with his breath,
And here, in his abode,
Light, wind, and air praise God,
And this poor breath.

Arthur Symons

114. PRAYERS

GOD who created me
    Nimble and light of limb,
In three elements free,
    To run, to ride, to swim :
Not when the sense is dim,
    But now from the heart of joy,
I would remember Him :
    Take the thanks of a boy.

Jesu, King and Lord,
    Whose are my foes to fight,

Gird me with Thy sword,
    Swift and sharp and bright.
Thee would I serve if I might ;
    And conquer if I can,
From day-dawn till night,
    Take the strength of a man.

Spirit of Love and Truth,
    Breathing in grosser clay,
The light and flame of youth,
    Delight of men in the fray,
Wisdom in strength's decay ;
    From pain, strife, wrong to be free,
This best gift I pray,
    Take my spirit to Thee.
Henry Charles Beeching.

115. THE SHEPHERDESS

SHE walks—the lady of my delight—
    A shepherdess of sheep.
Her flocks are thoughts. She keeps them white ;
    She guards them from the steep ;
She feeds them on the fragrant height,
    And folds them in for sleep.

She roams maternal hills and bright,
    Dark valleys safe and deep.
Into that tender breast at night
    The chastest stars may peep.
She walks—the lady of my delight—
    A shepherdess of sheep.

She holds her little thoughts in sight,
    Though gay they run and leap.
She is so circumspect and right ;
    She has her soul to keep.
She walks—the lady of my delight—
    A shepherdess of sheep.

Alice Meynell.

116. GIBBERISH

MANY a flower have I seen blossom,
    Many a bird for me will sing.
Never heard I so sweet a singer,
    Never saw I so fair a thing.

She is a bird, a bird that blossoms,
    She is a flower, a flower that sings ;
And I a flower when I behold her,
    And when I hear her, I have wings.

Mary E. Coleridge.

117. MARTHA

" ONCE . . . once upon a time . . .
    Over and over again,
Martha would tell us her stories,
    In the hazel glen.

Hers were those clear grey eyes
    You watch, and the story seems
Told by their beautifulness
    Tranquil as dreams.

She'd sit with her two slim hands
    Clasped round her bended knees ;
While we on our elbows lolled,
    And stared at ease.

Her voice and her narrow chin,
    Her grave small lovely head,
Seemed half the meaning
    Of the words she said.

" Once . . . once upon a time . . ."
    Like a dream you dream in the night,
Fairies and gnomes stole out
    In the leaf-green light.

And her beauty far away
    Would fade, as her voice ran on,
Till hazel and summer sun
    And all were gone :—

All fordone and forgot ;
    And like clouds in the height of the sky,
Our hearts stood still in the hush
    Of an age gone by.

                    Walter de la Mare.

118. A FRIEND

ALL, that he came to give,
    He gave, and went again :
I have seen one man live,
I have seen one man reign,
With all the graces in his train.

As one of us, he wrought
Things of the common hour :
Whence was the charmed soul brought,
That gave each act such power ;
The natural beauty of a flower ?

Magnificence and grace,
Excellent courtesy :
A brightness on the face,
Airs of high memory :
Whence came all these, to such as he ?

Like young Shakespearian kings,
He won the adoring throng :
And, as Apollo sings,
He triumphed with a song :
Triumphed, and sang, and passed along.

With a light word, he took
The hearts of men in thrall :
And, with a golden look,
Welcomed them, at his call
Giving their love, their strength, their all.

No man less proud than he,
Nor cared for homage less :
Only, he could not be
Far off from happiness :
Nature was bound to his success.

.T.D. I—5*

Weary, the cares, the jars,
The lets, of every day,
But the heavens filled with stars,
Chanced he upon the way :
And where he stayed, all joy would stay.

Now, when sad night draws down,
When the austere stars burn :
Roaming the vast live town,
My thoughts and memories yearn
Toward him, who never will return.

Yet have I seen him live,
And owned my friend, a king :
All that he came to give
He gave : and I, who sing
His praise, bring all I have to bring.

Lionel Johnson.

119. TWILIGHT

TWILIGHT it is, and the far woods are dim, and the
rooks cry and call.
Down in the valley the lamps, and the mist, and a
star over all,
There by the rick, where they thresh, is the drone at
an end,
Twilight it is, and I travel the road with my friend.

I think of the friends who are dead, who were dear
long ago in the past,
Beautiful friends who are dead, though I know that
death cannot last ;

Friends with the beautiful eyes that the dust has
     defiled,
Beautiful souls who were gentle when I was a child.
                              John Masefield.

120. ON THE DEATH OF ARNOLD TOYNBEE

GOOD-BYE ; no tears nor cries
     Are fitting here, and long lament were vain.
  Only the last low words be softly said,
  And the last greeting given above the dead ;
For soul more pure and beautiful our eyes
     Never shall see again.

     Alas ! what help is it,
What consolation in this heavy chance,
  That to the blameless life so soon laid low
  This was the end appointed long ago,
This the allotted space, the measure fit
     Of endless ordinance ?

     Thus were the ancient days
Made like our own monotonous with grief ;
  From unassuagèd lips even thus hath flown
  Perpetually the immemorial moan
Of those that weeping went on desolate ways,
     Nor found in tears relief.

     For faces yet grow pale,
Tears rise at fortune, and true hearts take fire
  In all who hear, with quickening pulse's stroke,
  That cry that from the infinite people broke,
When third among them Helen led the wail
     At Hector's funeral pyre.

And by the Latin beach
At rise of dawn such piteous tears were shed,
     When Troy and Arcady in long array
     Followed the princely body on its way,
And Lord Aeneas spoke the last sad speech
     Above young Pallas dead.

     Even in this English clime
The same sweet cry no circling seas can drown,
     In melancholy cadence rose to swell
     Some dirge of Lycidas or Astrophel
When lovely souls and pure before their time
     Into the dusk went down.

     These Earth, the bounteous nurse,
Hath long ago lapped in deep peace divine.
     Lips that made musical their old-world woe
     Themselves have gone to silence long ago,
And left a weaker voice and wearier verse,
     O royal soul, for thine.

     Beyond our life how far
Soars his new life through radiant orb and zone,
     While we in impotency of the night
     Walk dumbly, and the path is hard, and light
Fails, and for sun and moon the single star
     Honour is left alone.

     The star that knows no set,
But circles ever with a fixed desire,
     Watching Orion's armour all of gold ;
     Watching and wearying not, till pale and cold
Dawn breaks, and the first shafts of morning fret
     The east with lines of fire.

But on the broad low plain
When night is clear and windy, with hard frost,
  Such as had once the morning in their eyes,
  Watching and wearying, gaze upon the skies,
And cannot see that star for their great pain
    Because the sun is lost.

    Alas, how all our love
Is scant at best to fill so ample room !
  Image and influence fall too fast away
  And fading memory cries at dusk of day
Deem'st thou the dust recks aught at all thereof,
    The ghost within the tomb ?

    For even o'er lives like his
The slumberous river washes soft and slow ;
  The lapping water rises wearily,
  Numbing the nerve and will to sleep ; and we
Before the goal and crown of mysteries
    Fall back, and dare not know.

    Only at times we know,
In gyres convolved and luminous orbits whirled
  The soul beyond her knowing seems to sweep
  Out of the deep, fire-winged, into the deep ;
As two, who loved each other here below
    Better than all the world.

    Yet ever held apart,
And never knew their own hearts' deepest things,
  After long lapse of periods, wandering far
  Beyond the pathways of the furthest star.
Into communicable space might dart
    With tremor of thunderous wings ;

Across the void might call
Each unto each past worlds that raced and ran,
    And flash through galaxies, and clasp and kiss
    In some slant chasm and infinite abyss
Far in the faint sidereal interval
        Between the Lyre and Swan.

J. W. Mackail.

121. ESTRANGEMENT

So, without overt breach, we fall apart,
    Tacitly sunder—neither you nor I
Conscious of one intelligible Why,
And both, from severance, winning equal smart.
So, with resigned and acquiescent heart,
Whene'er your name on some chance lip may lie,
I seem to see an alien shade pass by,
A spirit wherein I have no lot or part.

Thus may a captive, in some fortress grim,
From casual speech betwixt his warders, learn
That June on her triumphant progress goes
Through arched and bannered woodlands; while for
    him
She is a legend emptied of concern,
And idle is the rumour of the rose.

William Watson.

122. FATHERHOOD

A kiss, a word of thanks, away
    They're gone, and you forsaken learn
The blessedness of giving; they
    (So Nature bids) forget, nor turn
    To where you sit, and watch, and yearn.

And you (so Nature bids) would go
  Through fire and water for their sake ;
Rise early, late take rest, to sow
  Their wealth, and lie all night awake
  If but their little finger ache.

The storied prince with wondrous hair
  Which stole men's heart and wrought his bale,
Rebelling, since he had no heir,
  Built him a pillar in the vale,
  —Absalom's—lest his name should fail.

It fails not, though the pillar lies
  In dust, because the outraged one,
His father, with strong agonies
  Cried it until the day was done—
  " O Absalom, my son, my son ! "

So Nature bade ; or might it be
  God, who in Jewry once (they say)
Cried with a great cry, " Come to me,
  Children," who still held on their way,
  Though He spread out His hands all day ?
                    Henry Charles Beeching.

123. DAISY

WHERE the thistle lifts a purple crown
      Six foot out of the turf,
And the harebell shakes on the windy hill—
  O the breath of the distant surf !—

The hills look over on the South,
　And southward dreams the sea ;
And with the sea-breeze hand in hand
　Came innocence and she.

Where 'mid the gorse the raspberry
　Red for the gatherer springs,
Two children did we stray and talk
　Wise, idle, childish things.

She listened with big-lipped surprise,
　Breast-deep 'mid flower and spine :
Her skin was like a grape, whose veins
　Run snow instead of wine.

She knew not those sweet words she spake,
　Nor knew her own sweet way ;
But there's never a bird, so sweet a song
　Thronged in whose throat that day.

Oh, there were flowers in Storrington
　On the turf and on the spray ;
But the sweetest flower on Sussex hills
　Was the Daisy-flower that day !

Her beauty smoothed earth's furrowed face ;
　She gave me tokens three :—
A look, a word of her winsome mouth,
　And a wild raspberry.

A berry red, a guileless look,
　A still word,—strings of sand !
And yet they made my wild, wild heart
　Fly down to her little hand.

For standing artless as the air,
  And candid as the skies,
She took the berries with her hand,
  And the love with her sweet eyes.

The fairest things have fleetest end,
  Their scent survives their close :
But the rose's scent is bitterness
  To him that loved the rose.

She looked a little wistfully,
  Then went her sunshine way :—
The sea's eye had a mist on it,
  And the leaves fell from the day.

She went her unremembering way,
  She went and left in me
The pang of all the partings gone,
  And partings yet to be.

She left me marvelling why my soul
  Was sad that she was glad ;
At all the sadness in the sweet,
  The sweetness in the sad.

Still, still I seemed to see her, still
  Look up with soft replies,
And take the berries with her hand,
  And the love with her lovely eyes.

Nothing begins, and nothing ends,
　　That is not paid with moan ;
For we are born in other's pain,
　　And perish in our own.

Francis Thompson.

124. A CRADLE SONG

O, MEN from the fields !
　　Come gently within.
Tread softly, softly,
　　O ! men coming in.

Mavourneen is going
　　From me and from you,
Where Mary will fold him
　　With mantle of blue !

From reek of the smoke
　　And cold of the floor,
And the peering of things
　　Across the half-door.

O, men from the fields !
　　Soft, softly come thro'.
Mary puts round him
　　Her mantle of blue.

Padraic Colum.

125. ON A DEAD CHILD

PERFECT little body, without fault or stain on thee,
　　With promise of strength and manhood full
and fair !

Though cold and stark and bare,
The bloom and the charm of life doth awhile remain
    on thee.

Thy mother's treasure wert thou ;—alas ! no longer
    To visit her heart with wondrous joy ; to be
        Thy father's pride ;—ah, he
Must gather his faith together, and his strength make
    stronger.

To me, as I move thee now in the last duty,
    Dost thou with a turn or gesture anon respond ;
        Startling my fancy fond
With a chance attitude of the head, a freak of beauty.

Thy hand clasps, as 'twas wont, my finger, and
    holds it :
    But the grasp is the clasp of Death, heartbreaking
        and stiff ;
        Yet feels to my hand as if
'Twas still thy will, thy pleasure and trust that
    enfolds it.

So I lay thee there, thy sunken eyelids closing,—
    Go, lie thou there in thy coffin, thy last little bed !—
        Propping thy wise, sad head,
Thy firm, pale hands across thy chest disposing.

So quiet ! doth the change content thee ?—Death,
    whither hath he taken thee ?
    To a world, do I think, that rights the disaster of
        this ?

The vision of which I miss,
Who weep for the body, and wish but to warm thee
    and awaken thee ?

Ah ! little at best can all our hopes avail us
    To lift this sorrow, or cheer us, when in the dark,
        Unwilling, alone we embark,
And the things we have seen and have known and
    have heard of, fail us.

Robert Bridges.

126. I NEVER SHALL LOVE THE SNOW AGAIN

I NEVER shall love the snow again
    Since Maurice died :
With corniced drift it blocked the lane,
And sheeted in a desolate plain
    The country side.

The trees with silvery rime bedight
    Their branches bare.
By day no sun appeared ; by night
The hidden moon shed thievish light
    In the misty air.

We fed the birds that flew around
    In flocks to be fed :
No shelter in holly or brake they found.
The speckled thrush on the frozen ground
    Lay frozen and dead.

We skated on stream and pond ; we cut
        The crinching snow
To Doric temple or Arctic hut ;
We laughed and sang at nightfall, shut
        By the fireside glow.

Yet grudged we our keen delights before
        Maurice should come.
We said, " In-door or out-of-door
We shall love life for a month or more,
        When he is home."

They brought him home ; 'twas two days late
        For Christmas Day :
Wrapped in white, in solemn state,
A flower in his hand, all still and straight
        Our Maurice lay.

And two days ere the year outgave
        We laid him low.
The best of us truly were not brave,
When we laid Maurice down in his grave
        Under the snow.

                                Robert Bridges.

127. TO MY GODCHILD

Francis M. W. M.

THIS labouring, vast, Tellurian galleon,
        Riding at anchor off the orient sun,
Had broken its cable, and stood out to space
Down some frore Arctic of the aërial ways :

And now, back warping from the inclement main,
Its vaporous shroudage drenched with icy rain,
It swung into its azure roads again ;
When, floated on the prosperous sun-gale, you
Lit, a white halcyon auspice, 'mid our frozen crew.

To the Sun, stranger, surely you belong,
Giver of golden days and golden song ;
Nor is it by an all-unhappy plan
You bear the name of me, his constant Magian.
Yet ah ! from any other that it came,
Lest fated to my fate you be, as to my name.
When at the first those tidings did they bring,
My heart turned troubled at the ominous thing :
Though well may such a title him endower,
For whom a poet's prayer implores a poet's power.
The Assisian, who kept plighted faith to three,
To Song, to Sanctitude, and Poverty,
(In two alone of whom most singers prove
A fatal faithfulness of during love !)
He the sweet Sales, of whom we scarcely ken
How God he could love more, he so loved men ;
The crown and crowned of Laura and Italy ;
And Fletcher's fellow—from these, and not from me.
Take you your name, and take your legacy !

Or, if a right successive you declare
When worms, for ivies, intertwine my hair,
Take but this Poesy that now followeth
My clayey hest with sullen servile breath,
Made then your happy freedman by testating death.

My song I do but hold for you in trust,
I ask you but to blossom from my dust.
When you have compassed all weak I began,
Diviner poet, and ah ! diviner man ;
The man at feud with the perduring child
In you before Song's altar nobly reconciled ;
From the wise heavens I half shall smile to see
How little a world, which owned you, needed me.
If, while you keep the vigils of the night,
For your wild tears make darkness all too bright,
Some lone orb through your lonely window peeps,
As it played lover over your sweet sleeps ;
Think it a golden crevice in the sky,
Which I have pierced but to behold you by !

And when, immortal mortal, droops your head,
And you, the child of deathless song, are dead ;
Then, as you search with unaccustomed glance
The ranks of Paradise for my countenance,
Turn not your tread along the Uranian sod
Among the bearded counsellors of God ;
For if in Eden as on earth are we,
I sure shall keep a younger company :
Pass where beneath their rangèd gonfalons
The starry cohorts shake their shielded suns,
The dreadful mass of their enridgèd spears ;
Pass where majestical the eternal peers,
The stately choice of the great Saintdom, meet—
A silvern segregation, globed complete
In sandalled shadow of the Triune feet ;
Pass by where wait, young poet-wayfarer,

Your cousined clusters, emulous to share
With you the roseal lightnings burning 'mid their
    hair ;
Pass the crystalline sea, the Lampads seven :—
Look for me in the nurseries of Heaven.

Francis Thompson.

128. WHEN JUNE IS COME

WHEN June is come, then all the day
    I'll sit with my love in the scented hay :
And watch the sunshot palaces high,
That the white clouds build in the breezy sky.

She singeth, and I do make her a song,
And read sweet poems the whole day long :
Unseen as we lie in our hay-built home.
Oh, life is delight when June is come.

Robert Bridges.

129. IN MISTY BLUE

IN misty blue the lark is heard
    Above the silent homes of men ;
The bright-eyed thrush, the little wren,
The yellow-billed sweet-voiced blackbird
Mid sallow blossoms blond as curd
Or silver oak boughs, carolling
With happy throat from tree to tree,
Sing into light this morn of spring
That sang my dear love home to me.

Be starry, buds of clustered white,
Around the dark waves of her hair !
The young fresh glory you prepare
Is like my ever-fresh delight
When she comes shining on my sight
With meeting eyes, with such a cheek
As colours fair like flushing tips
Of shoots, and music ere she speak
Lies in the wonder of her lips.

Airs of the morning, breathe about
Keen faint scents of the wild wood side
From thickets where primroses hide
Mid the brown leaves of winter's rout.
Chestnut and willow, beacon out
For joy of her, from far and nigh,
Your English green on English hills :
Above her head, song-quivering sky,
And at her feet, the daffodils.

Because she breathed, the world was more,
And breath a finer soul to use,
And life held lovelier hopes to choose
But O, to-day my heart brims o'er,
Earth glows as from a kindled core,
Like shadows of diviner things
Are hill and cloud and flower and tree—
A splendour that is hers and spring's,—
The day my love came home to me.

Laurence Binyon.

130. IN FOUNTAIN COURT

THE fountain murmuring of sleep,
 A drowsy tune ;
The flickering green of leaves that keep
 The light of June ;
Peace, through a slumbering afternoon,
 The peace of June.

A waiting ghost, in the blue sky,
 The white curved moon ;
June, hushed and breathless, waits, and I
 Wait, too, with June ;
Come, through the lingering afternoon,
 Soon, love, come soon.

      Arthur Symons.

131. THE PRAISE OF DUST

" WHAT of vile dust ? " the preacher said.
 Methought the whole world woke,
The dead stone lived beneath my foot,
 And my whole body spoke.

" You that play tyrant to the dust,
 And stamp its wrinkled face,
This patient star that flings you not
 Far into homeless space,

" Come down out of your dusty shrine
 The living dust to see,
The flowers that at your sermon's end
 Stand blazing silently,

" Rich white and blood-red blossom ; stones,
  Lichens like fire encrust ;
A gleam of blue, a glare of gold,
  The vision of the dust.

" Pass them all by ; till, as you come
  Where, at a city's edge,
Under a tree—I know it well—
  Under a lattice ledge,

" The sunshine falls on one brown head.
  You, too, O cold of clay,
Eater of stones, may haply hear
  The trumpets of that day

" When God to all his paladins
  By his own splendour swore
To make a fairer face than heaven,
  Of dust and nothing more."

G. K. Chesterton.

132. AWAKE, MY HEART, TO BE LOVED

AWAKE, my heart, to be loved, awake, awake !
    The darkness silvers away, the morn doth break,
It leaps in the sky : unrisen lustres slake
The o'ertaken moon. Awake, O heart, awake !

She too that loveth awaketh and hopes for thee ;
Her eyes already have sped the shades that flee,

Already they watch the path thy feet shall take :
Awake, O heart, to be loved, awake, awake !

And if thou tarry from her,—if this could be,—
She cometh herself, O heart, to be loved, to thee ;
For thee would unashamèd herself forsake :
Awake to be loved, my heart, awake, awake !

Awake ! the land is scattered with light, and see,
Uncanopied sleep is flying from field and tree :
And blossoming boughs of April in laughter shake :
Awake, O heart, to be loved, awake, awake !

Lo all things wake and tarry and look for thee :
She looketh and saith, " O sun, now bring him to me.
Come more adored, O adored, for his coming's sake,
And awake my heart to be loved : awake, awake ! "
Robert Bridges.

133. AEDH WISHES FOR THE CLOTHS OF HEAVEN

Had I the heavens' embroidered cloths,
    Enwrought with golden and silver light,
The blue and the dim and the dark cloths
Of night and light and the half light,
I would spread the cloths under your feet :
But I, being poor, have only my dreams ;
I have spread my dreams under your feet ;
Tread softly because you tread on my dreams.
W. B. Yeats.

134. BEAUTY

I HAVE seen dawn and sunset on moors and windy
hills
Coming in solemn beauty like slow old tunes of Spain :
I have seen the lady April bringing the daffodils,
Bringing the springing grass and the soft warm April
rain.

I have heard the song of the blossoms and the old
chant of the sea,
And seen strange lands from under the arched white
sails of ships ;
But the loveliest things of beauty God ever has
showed to me,
Are her voice, and her hair, and eyes, and the dear red
curve of her lips.

John Masefield.

135. MY WIFE

TRUSTY, dusky, vivid, true,
With eyes of gold and bramble-dew,
Steel-true and blade-straight,
The great artificer
Made my mate.

Honour, anger, valour, fire ;
A love that life could never tire,
Death quench or evil stir,
The mighty master
Gave to her.

Teacher, tender, comrade, wife,
A fellow-farer true through life,
Heart-whole and soul-free
The august father
Gave to me.

Robert Louis Stevenson.

136. FROM "LOVE IN THE VALLEY"

SHY as the squirrel and wayward as the swallow,
    Swift as the swallow along the river's light
Circleting the surface to meet his mirrored winglets,
    Fleeter she seems in her stay than in her flight.
Shy as the squirrel that leaps among the pine-tops,
    Wayward as the swallow overhead at set of sun,
She whom I love is hard to catch and conquer,
    Hard, but O the glory of the winning were she won !

   *   *   *   *   *

Heartless she is as the shadow in the meadows
    Flying to the hills on a blue and breezy noon.
No, she is athirst and drinking up her wonder :
    Earth to her is young as the slip of the new moon.
Deals she an unkindness, 'tis but her rapid measure,
    Even as in a dance ; and her smile can heal no less :
Like the swinging May-cloud that pelts the flowers
        with hailstones
    Off a sunny border, she was made to bruise and
        bless.

   *   *   *   *   *

Stepping down the hill with her fair companions,
    Arm in arm, all against the raying West,

Boldly she sings, to the merry tune she marches,
    Brave is her shape, and sweeter unpossessed.
Sweeter, for she is what my heart first awaking
    Whispered the world was ; morning light is she.
Love that so desires would fain keep her changeless ;
    Fain would fling the net, and fain have her free.

      *   *   *   *   *

Happy, happy time, when the white star hovers
    Low over dim fields fresh with bloomy dew,
Near the face of dawn, that draws athwart the dark-
      ness,
    Threading it with colour, like yewberries the yew.
Thicker crowd the shades as the grave East deepens,
    Glowing, and with crimson a long cloud swells.
Maiden still the morn is ; and strange she is, and
      secret ;
    Strange her eyes ; her cheeks are cold as cold sea-
      shells.

      *   *   *   *   *

Peering at her chamber the white crowns the red rose,
    Jasmine winds the porch with stars two and three.
Parted is the window ; she sleeps ; the starry jasmine
    Breathes a falling breath that carries thoughts of
      me.
Sweeter unpossessed, have I said of her my sweetest ?
    Not while she sleeps : while she sleeps the jasmine
      breathes,
Luring her to love ; she sleeps ; the starry jasmine
    Bears me to her pillow under white rose-wreaths.
                         George Meredith.

137. TO THE BELOVED

OH, not more subtly silence strays
    Amongst the winds, between the voices,
Mingling alike with pensive lays,
    And with the music that rejoices,
Than thou art present in my days.

My silence, life returns to thee
    In all the pauses of her breath.
Hush back to rest the melody
    That out of thee awakeneth ;
And thou, wake ever, wake for me !

Thou art like silence all unvexed,
    Though wild words part my soul from thee.
Thou art like silence unperplexed,
    A secret and a mystery
Between one footfall and the next.

Most dear pause in a mellow lay !
    Thou art inwoven with every air.
With thee the wildest tempests play,
    And snatches of thee everywhere
Make little heavens throughout a day.

Darkness and solitude shine, for me.
    For life's fair outward part are rife
The silver noises ; let them be.
    It is the very soul of life
Listens for thee, listens for thee.

O pause between the sobs of cares ;
　　O thought within all thought that is ;
Trance between laughters unawares :
　　Thou art the shape of melodies,
And thou the ecstasy of prayers !

Alice Meynell.

138. WHEN YOU ARE OLD

WHEN you are old and gray and full of sleep,
　　And nodding by the fire, take down this
　　book,
And slowly read, and dream of the soft look
Your eyes had once, and of their shadows deep ;

How many loved your moments of glad grace,
And loved your beauty with love false or true ;
But one man loved the pilgrim soul in you,
And loved the sorrows of your changing face.

And bending down beside the glowing bars
Murmur, a little sadly, how love fled
And paced upon the mountains overhead
And hid his face amid a crowd of stars.

W. B. Yeats.

139. I WILL NOT LET THEE GO

I WILL not let thee go.
　　Ends all our month-long love in this ?
　　Can it be summed up so,
　　Quit in a single kiss ?
　　I will not let thee go.

P.T.D. I—6

I will not let thee go.
If thy words' breath could scare thy deeds,
As the soft south can blow
And toss the feathered seeds,
Then might I let thee go.

I will not let thee go.
Had not the great sun seen, I might ;
Or were he reckoned slow
To bring the false to light,
Then might I let thee go.

I will not let thee go.
The stars that crowd the summer skies
Have watched us so below
With all their million eyes,
I dare not let thee go.

I will not let thee go.
Have we not chid the changeful moon,
Now rising late, and now
Because she set too soon,
And shall I let thee go ?

I will not let thee go.
Have not the young flowers been content,
Plucked ere their buds could blow,
To seal our sacrament ?
I cannot let thee go.

I will not let thee go.
I hold thee by too many bands :
Thou sayest farewell, and lo !
I have thee by the hands,
And will not let thee go.

Robert Bridges.

140. PARTED

FAREWELL to one now silenced quite,
Sent out of hearing, out of sight,—
My friend of friends, whom I shall miss.
He is not banished, though, for this,—
Nor he, nor sadness, nor delight.

Though I shall talk with him no more,
A low voice sounds upon the shore.
He must not watch my resting-place,
But who shall drive a mournful face
From the sad winds about my door ?

I shall not hear his voice complain,
But who shall stop the patient rain ?
His tears must not disturb my heart,
But who shall change the years, and part
The world from every thought of pain ?

Although my life is left so dim,
The morning crowns the mountain-rim ;
Joy is not gone from summer skies,
Nor innocence from children's eyes,
And all these things are part of him.

He is not banished, for the showers
Yet wake this green warm earth of ours.
How can the summer but be sweet ?
I shall not have him at my feet,
And yet my feet are on the flowers.

Alice Meynell.

141. ELEGY ON A LADY, WHOM GRIEF FOR THE DEATH OF HER BETROTHED KILLED

A SSEMBLE, all ye maidens, at the door,
And all ye loves, assemble ; far and wide
Proclaim the bridal, that proclaimed before
Has been deferred to this late eventide :
For on this night the bride,
The days of her betrothal over,
Leaves the parental hearth for evermore ;
To-night the bride goes forth to meet her lover.

Reach down the wedding vesture, that has lain
Yet all unvisited, the silken gown :
Bring out the bracelets, and the golden chain
Her dearer friends provided : sere and brown
Bring out the festal crown,
And set it on her forehead lightly :
Though it be withered, twine no wreath again ;
This only is the crown she can wear rightly.

Cloak her in ermine, for the night is cold,
And wrap her warmly, for the night is long ;
In pious hands the flaming torches hold,
While her attendants, chosen from among

Her faithful virgin throng,
May lay her in her cedar litter,
Decking her coverlet with sprigs of gold,
Roses, and lilies white that best befit her.

Sound flute and tabor, that the bridal be
Not without music, nor with these alone ;
But let the viol lead the melody,
With lesser intervals, and plaintive moan
    Of sinking semitone ;
    And, all in choir, the virgin voices
Rest not from singing in skilled harmony
The song that aye the bridegroom's ear rejoices.

Let the priests go before, arrayed in white,
And let the dark-stoled minstrels follow slow,
Next they that bear her, honoured on this night,
And then the maidens, in a double row,
    Each singing soft and low,
    And each on high a torch upstaying :
Unto her lover lead her forth with light,
With music, and with singing, and with praying.

'Twas at this sheltering hour he nightly came,
And found her trusty window open wide,
And knew the signal of the timorous flame,
That long the restless curtain would not hide
    Her form that stood beside ;
    As scarce she dared to be delighted,
Listening to that sweet tale, that is no shame
To faithful lovers, that their hearts have plighted.

But now for many days the dewy grass
Has shown no markings of his feet at morn :
And watching she has seen no shadow pass
The moonlit walk, and heard no music borne
        Upon her ear forlorn.
    In vain she has looked out to greet him ;
    He has not come, he will not come, alas !
So let us bear her out where she must meet him.

Now to the river bank the priests are come :
The bark is ready to receive its freight :
Let some prepare her place therein, and some
Embark the litter with its slender weight :
        The rest stand by in state,
        And sing her a safe passage over ;
    While she is oared across to her new home,
Into the arms of her expectant lover.

And thou, O lover, that art on the watch,
Where, on the banks of the forgetful streams,
The pale indifferent ghosts wander, and snatch
The sweeter moments of their broken dreams,—
        Thou, when the torchlight gleams,
        When thou shalt see the slow procession,
    And when thine ears the fitful music catch,
Rejoice, for thou art near to thy possession.
                                    Robert Bridges.

142. AN EPITAPH

HERE lies a most beautiful lady,
　　Light of step and heart was she ;
I think she was the most beautiful lady
That ever was in the West Country.
But beauty vanishes ; beauty passes ;
However rare—rare it be ;
And when I crumble, who will remember
This lady of the West Country ?

Walter de la Mare.

143 A DREAM OF DEATH

I DREAMED that one had died in a strange place
　　Near no accustomed hand ;
And they had nailed the boards above her face,
The peasants of that land,
And, wondering, planted by her solitude
A cypress and a yew :
I came, and wrote upon a cross of wood,
Man had no more to do :
She was more beautiful than thy first love,
This lady by the trees :
And gazed upon the mournful stars above,
And heard the mournful breeze.

W. B. Yeats.

144. A DREAM OF A BLESSED SPIRIT

ALL the heavy days are over ;
　　Leave the body's coloured pride
Underneath the grass and clover,
With the feet laid side by side.

One with her are mirth and duty;
Bear the gold embroidered dress,
For she needs not her sad beauty,
To the scented oaken press.

Hers the kiss of Mother Mary,
The long hair is on her face;
Still she goes with footsteps wary,
Full of earth's old timid grace:

With white feet of angels seven
Her white feet go glimmering;
And above the deep of heaven,
Flame on flame and wing on wing.

W. B. Yeats.

145. MESSAGES

WHAT shall I your true-love tell,
　　Earth-forsaking maid?
What shall I your true-love tell,
　　When life's spectre's laid?

" Tell him that, our side the grave,
　　Maid may not conceive
Life should be so sad to have,
　　That's so sad to leave! "

What shall I your true-love tell,
　　When I come to him?
What shall I your true-love tell—
　　Eyes growing dim!

"Tell him this, when you shall part
    From a maiden pined ;
That I see him with my heart,
    Now my eyes are blind."

What shall I your true-love tell ?
    Speaking-while is scant.
What shall I your true-love tell,
    Death's white postulant ?

"Tell him—love, with speech at strife,
    For last utterance saith :
I, who loved with all my life,
    Love with all my death."

                              Francis Thompson.

146. THE FOLLY OF BEING COMFORTED

ONE that is ever kind said yesterday :
    " Your well-beloved's hair has threads of grey,
And little shadows come about her eyes ;
Time can but make it easier to be wise,
Though now it's hard, till trouble is at an end ;
And so be patient, be wise and patient, friend."
But, heart, there is no comfort, not a grain ;
Time can but make her beauty over again,
Because of that great nobleness of hers ;
The fire that stirs about her, when she stirs
Burns but more clearly.   O she had not these ways,
When all the wild summer was in her gaze.
O heart !   O heart ! if she'd but turn her head,
You'd know the folly of being comforted.

                              W. B. Yeats.

147. AT NIGHT

To W. M.

HOME, home from the horizon far and clear,
  Hither the soft wings sweep ;
Flocks of the memories of the day draw near
  The dovecote doors of sleep.

Oh, which are they that come through sweetest light
  Of all these homing birds ?
Which with the straightest and the swiftest flight ?
  Your words to me, your words !

Alice Meynell.

INDEX OF FIRST LINES

Poems of To-Day:

Second Series

Poems of To-Day:

Second Series

London:
Published for the English Association
by Sidgwick & Jackson, Ltd.

First issued in May, **1922**
Reprinted, July and September, 1922
January and September, 1923
January and November, 1924
August and October, 1925
June and July, 1928
July and August, 1929
May, 1931
May, 1933
May and October, 1934
May, 1936
July, 1941
September, **1942**
April, 1943
October, 1943
April, 1944
October, 1945
August, 1946
September, 1947
October, 1948
November, **1951**
April, 1954
September, 1959

PRINTED AND BOUND IN ENGLAND BY
HAZELL WATSON AND VINEY LTD
AYLESBURY AND SLOUGH

PREFATORY NOTE

THE welcome accorded to the first volume of "Poems of To-day" leads the Committee to hope that a second volume may be of service to those interested in the poetry of their own times. The first volume was published in August, 1915; the interval that has passed has brought to all experience which the imagination of a few has transmuted into poetry. This second volume is an attempt to bring together such poems as represent, not indeed all the shifting tendencies of the period, but those moods which have proved most permanent, persisting through all the changes of events and of public feeling, linking the poetry of to-day with that of yesterday, and looking forward to the poetry of to-morrow.

Most of the selections are from the writings of younger men, who have written mainly under the influences and reactions of the war; but others are from the works of older and more established poets who have not lost touch with this generation. Living poets whose outlook and method belong to the earlier rather than to the second decade of the century do not come within the scope of the anthology, but poems by writers now dead have been admitted, where for reasons of copyright such writers were excluded from the first volume or inadequately represented there.

For the choice and arrangement of the poems, the war necessarily provides the starting-point. The moods of war are shown, occasionally as they have been realised in the first crude shock of actual encounter, but more often as they have been deepened and stabilised in the impassioned memories of the poet. From the war, men's minds have turned to England, sometimes with pride in her past, sometimes with doubt for her future, but never with despair. The poets have paid tribute to the hold upon them of school and college and home, of green countryside and rolling downland, of heroic memories and well-loved associations. The poetry of nature shows a strength of local feeling that escapes from the limits of provincial sentiment by its unassuming but deep-rooted sincerity. With the love of nature is found a sympathy with animals half-humorous, half tender. The sense of fellowship and the love of life are the more marked because of the events which have threatened both, but love between man and woman is a less distinctive note in the poetry of the day. Romance is blended with realism, and escape is made from modern conventions and modern conditions, sometimes by looking back into the past, more often by way of the sea and far wanderings, sometimes by magic. Finally, the mystery of death has quickened men's perception of the mystery of life and of the immanence of spirit.

January, 1922.

INDEX OF AUTHORS

For permission to use copyright poems, the English Association is greatly indebted to the authors; to the literary executors of F. W. Bourdillon (Mrs. Bourdillon), Rupert Brooke (Mr. E. H. Marsh), T. E. Brown (Mrs. Brown), A. H. Bullen (Miss E. Lister), "Michael Field" (Mr. T. Sturge Moore), J. E. Flecker (Mrs. Flecker), Julian Grenfell (Lady Desborough), W. N. Hodgson (Miss Hodgson), Francis Ledwidge (Lord Dunsany), F. W. Moorman (Mrs. Moorman), J. M. Plunkett (Mrs. Plunkett), C. H. Sorley (Professor W. R. Sorley), Sir Cecil Spring-Rice (Mr. Bernard Holland), E. Wyndham Tennant (Lady Glenconner), Edward Thomas (Mrs. Thomas), Francis Thompson (Mr. Wilfrid Meynell), and T. P. Cameron Wilson (Rev. T. Wilson); and to the following publishers in respect of the poems enumerated:

Messrs. Allen & Unwin:
   Beatrice Mayor, *Poems* (No. 39).
   Gilbert Murray, *The Hippolytus of Euripides* (No. 115).

Messrs. G. Bell & Sons, Ltd.:
   Michael Field, *Callirrhoë and Fair Rosamund* (No. 76).

Mr. Basil Blackwell:
   Aldous Huxley, *The Defeat of Youth* (No. 53).
   M. Nightingale, *Verses Wise and Otherwise* (No. 124).
   E. W. Tennant, *Worple Flit* (No. 10).

Messrs. W. Blackwood & Sons:
   Moira O'Neill, *Songs of the Glens of Antrim* (No. 64).

Messrs. Burns, Oates & Washbourne, Ltd.:
   G. K. Chesterton, *Poems* (No. 98).
   Alice Meynell, *Poems* (Nos. 93, 138).
   F. Thompson, *Poetry of* (Nos. 30, 78, 139, 140).

Messrs. Chatto & Windus:
   Aldous Huxley, *Leda* (No. 31).
   Robert Nichols, *Ardours and Endurances* (Nos. 1, 5, 7, 9).

Messrs. W. Collins Sons & Co., Ltd. :
  E. Shanks, *The Island of Youth* (No. 38).

Messrs. Constable & Co., Ltd. :
  F. S. Boas, *Songs of Ulster and Balliol* (No. 58).
  W. de la Mare, *Collected Poems* (Nos. 27, 41, 122, 128).
  M. C. Furse, *The Gift* (No. 29).
  R. Macaulay, *Three Days* (No. 49).
  Lady Margaret Sackville, *Selected Poems* (No. 108).

Messrs. J. M. Dent & Sons, Ltd. :
  G. K. Chesterton, *The Wild Knight* (No. 71).
  Evelyn Underhill, *Immanence* (Nos. 129, 130).
  J. E. Flecker, *Forty-two Poems* (No. 119).

Messrs. Duckworth & Co. :
  H. Belloc, *Verses* (No. 102).

Mr. W. Heinemann :
  Robert Bridges, *October and other Poems* (No. 99).
  G. Dearmer, *Poems* (No. 75).
  J. Galsworthy, *Moods, Songs, and Doggerels* (No. 51).
  S. Sassoon, *War Poems* (No. 35).

Messrs. Herbert Jenkins, Ltd. :
  F. Ledwidge, *Songs of Peace* (No. 47), and
                Songs of the Fields (No. 120).

Messrs. John Lane, Ltd. :
  E. A. Mackintosh, *The Highland Regiment* (No. 2).

Messrs. Longmans, Green & Co. :
  Eva Gore-Booth, *The One and the Many* (No. 62).
  Sir C. Spring-Rice, *Collected Poems.* ed. B. Holland (Nos. 24, 101).

Messrs. Macmillan & Co., Ltd. :
  A. E. (George Russell), *Collected Poems* (Nos. 23, 63, 132, 133)
  T. E. Brown, *Collected Poems* (Nos. 42, 97, 109).
  W. W. Gibson, *Whin* (No. 20).
  Thomas Hardy, *Collected Poems* (Nos. 22, 67, 81, 121).
  R. Hodgson, *Poems* (Nos. 40, 69, 134).
  S. R. Lysaght, *Horizons and Landmarks* (No. 44), and
                  Poems of the Unknown Way (No. 91).
  James Stephens, *Adventures of Seumas Beg* (Nos. 65), and
                   Songs from the Clay (Nos. 70, 85).

Mr. Elkin Mathews :
  L. Binyon, *The Four Years* (Nos. 12, 17).
  G. Bottomley, *Chambers of Imagery, 2nd Series* (Nos. 33, 55).
  W. W. Gibson, *Fires* (No. 104).
  F. W. Moorman, *Songs of the Ridings* (No. 89).

Messrs. Maunsel & Roberts, Ltd. :
  P. Colum, *Wild Earth* (Nos. 83, 90).
  S. O'Sullivan, *Poems* (No. 106).
  James Stephens, *Insurrections* (Nos. 86, 107).

Messrs. Methuen & Co., Ltd. :
    Herbert Trench, *Deirdre Wed, and other Poems* (No. 79).

Mr. John Murray :
    R. Bridges, *Poetical Works* (Nos. 50, 110).
    W. N. Hodgson, *Verse and Prose in Peace and War* (Nos. 3, 11, 26).
    Violet Jacob, *Songs of Angus* (Nos. 87, 88).
    W. M. Letts, *Songs from Leinster* (No. 74).
    Sir H. Newbolt, *Poems* (Nos. 13, 16, 113, 137).

Messrs. Grant Richards, Ltd. :
    T. Sturge Moore, *The Little School* (Nos. 28, 77).

Messrs. Martin Secker, Ltd. :
    Maurice Baring, *Poems* 1914–1919 (No. 19).
    J. E. Flecker, *Collected Poems* (Nos. 21, 54, 111).

Messrs. Selwyn & Blount, Ltd. :
    J. Freeman, *Poems New and Old* (Nos. 25, 61).
    E. Thomas, *Poems* (Nos. 46, 48, 84).

Messrs. Sidgwick & Jackson, Ltd. :
    H. Asquith, *The Volunteer* (Nos. 6, 15).
    E. Blunden, *The Waggoner* (Nos. 36, 45).
    R. Brooke, *Collected Poems* (No. 96).
    A. H. Bullen, *Weeping-Cross* (Nos. 56, 105).
    J. Drinkwater, *Tides* (No. 37),
                 Poems, 1908–1914 (No. 59),
                 Olton Pools (No. 60), and
                 Loyalties (No. 68).
    F. W. Harvey, *Gloucestershire Friends* (No. 131), and
                 Ducks (No. 34).
    W. J. Turner, *The Dark Fire* (No. 117), and
                 The Hunter (No. 118).

The Talbot Press :
    Joseph Plunkett, *Collected Poems* (No. 135).

Messrs. T. Fisher Unwin, Ltd. :
    W. B. Yeats, *Poems* (Nos. 82, 126, 127).

Mr. J. G. Wilson :
    M. Caron Rock, *Or in the Grass* (No. 136).

The Poetry Bookshop (through Mr. Harold Monro) :
    Charlotte Mew, *The Farmer's Bride* (No. 123).
    H. Monro, *Children of Love* (No. 72), and
                 Strange Meetings (No. 100).
    T. P. Cameron Wilson, *Magpies in Picardy* (No. 125).

No. 66 is an early version of a poem by Mr. Herbert Trench appearing in the third edition of his *Poems with Fables in Prose* (Constable & Co. Ltd.)

The Editor of *The Westminster Gazette* courteously confirmed the authors' permissions in respect of Nos. 32, 80, and 94; and the Editor of *The Spectator* gave permission in respect of No. 8.

POEMS OF TO-DAY

SECOND SERIES

1. FAREWELL TO PLACE OF COMFORT

For the last time, maybe, upon the knoll
　　I stand.　The eve is golden, languid, sad . . .
Day like a tragic actor plays his rôle
To the last whispered word, and falls gold-clad.
I, too, take leave of all I ever had.

They shall not say I went with heavy heart :
Heavy I am, but soon I shall be free ;
I love them all, but oh ! I now depart
A little sadly, strangely, fearfully,
As one who goes to try a Mystery.

The bell is sounding down in Dedham Vale :
Be still, O bell ! too often standing here
When all the air was tremulous, fine, and pale,
Thy golden note so calm, so still, so clear,
Out of my stony heart has struck a tear.

And now tears are not mine.　I have release
From all the former and the later pain ;
Like the mid-sea I rock in boundless peace,

Soothed by the charity of the deep sea rain. . . .
Calm rain ! Calm sea ! Calm found, long sought in
    vain.

O bronzen pines, evening of gold and blue,
Steep mellow slope, brimmed twilit pools below,
Hushed trees, still vale dissolving in the dew,
Farewell ! Farewell ! There is no more to do.
We have been happy.   Happy now I go.
Robert Nichols.

2. CHA TILL MACCRUIMEIN

(*Departure of the 4th Camerons*)

THE pipes in the streets were playing bravely,
    The marching lads went by,
With merry hearts and voices singing
    My friends marched out to die ;
But I was hearing a lonely pibroch
    Out of an older war,
" Farewell, farewell, farewell, MacCrimmon,
    MacCrimmon comes no more."

And every lad in his heart was dreaming
    Of honour and wealth to come,
And honour and noble pride were calling
    To the tune of the pipes and drum :
But I was hearing a woman singing
    On dark Dunvegan shore,
" In battle or peace, with wealth or honour,
    MacCrimmon comes no more."

And there in front of the men were marching,
  With feet that made no mark,
The grey old ghosts of the ancient fighters
  Come back again from the dark ;
And in front of them all MacCrimmon piping
  A weary tune and sore,
" On the gathering day, for ever and ever,
  MacCrimmon comes no more."

Ewart Alan Mackintosh.

3. BEFORE ACTION

BY all the glories of the day
  And the cool evening's benison,
By that last sunset touch that lay
  Upon the hills when day was done,
By beauty lavishly outpoured
  And blessings carelessly received,
  By all the days that I have lived,
Make me a soldier, Lord.

By all of all man's hopes and fears,
  And all the wonders poets sing,
The laughter of unclouded years,
  And every sad and lovely thing ;
By the romantic ages stored
  With high endeavour that was his,
  By all his mad catastrophes,
Make me a man, O Lord.

I, that on my familiar hill
  Saw with uncomprehending eyes

A hundred of Thy sunsets spill
    Their fresh and sanguine sacrifice,
Ere the sun swings his noonday sword
    Must say good-bye to all of this ;—
    By all delights that I shall miss,
Help me to die, O Lord.

William Noel Hodgson.

4. INTO BATTLE

THE naked earth is warm with spring,
    And with green grass and bursting trees
Leans to the sun's gaze glorying,
    And quivers in the sunny breeze ;
And life is colour and warmth and light,
    And a striving evermore for these ;
And he is dead who will not fight ;
    And who dies fighting has increase.

The fighting man shall from the sun
    Take warmth, and life from the glowing earth ;
Speed with the light-foot winds to run,
    And with the trees to newer birth ;
And find, when fighting shall be done,
    Great rest, and fullness after dearth.

All the bright company of Heaven
    Hold him in their high comradeship,
The Dog-Star, and the Sisters Seven,
    Orion's Belt and sworded hip.

The woodland trees that stand together,
   They stand to him each one a friend ;
They gently speak in the windy weather ;
   They guide to valley and ridge's end.

The kestrel hovering by day,
   And the little owls that call by night,
Bid him be swift and keen as they,
   As keen of ear, as swift of sight.

The blackbird sings to him, " Brother, brother,
   If this be the last song you shall sing,
Sing well, for you may not sing another ;
   Brother, sing."

In dreary, doubtful, waiting hours,
   Before the brazen frenzy starts,
The horses show him nobler powers ;
   O patient eyes, courageous hearts !

And when the burning moment breaks,
   And all things else are out of mind,
And only joy of battle takes
   Him by the throat, and makes him blind,

Through joy and blindness he shall know,
   Not caring much to know, that still
Nor lead nor steel shall reach him, so
   That it be not the Destined Will.

The thundering line of battle stands,
   And in the air death moans and sings ;

But Day shall clasp him with strong hands,
And Night shall fold him in soft wings.

Julian Grenfell.

5. THE ASSAULT

THE beating of the guns grows louder.
" *Not long, boys, now.*"
My heart burns whiter, fearfuller, prouder.
Hurricanes grow
As guns redouble their fire.
Through the shaken periscope peeping,
I glimpse their wire :
Black earth, fountains of earth rise, leaping,
Spouting like shocks of meeting waves,
Death's fountains are playing,
Shells like shrieking birds rush over ;
Crash and din rises higher.
A stream of lead raves
Over us from the left . . . (we safe under cover !)
Crash !   Reverberation !   Crash !
Acrid smoke billowing.   Flash upon flash.
Black smoke drifting.   The German line
Vanishes in confusion, smoke.   Cries, and cry
Of our men, " *Gah, yer swine !*
Ye're for it," die
In a hurricane of shell.

One cry :
" *We're comin' soon ! look out !* "
There is opened hell
Over there ; fragments fly,

Rifles and bits of men whirled at the sky :
Dust, smoke, thunder ! A sudden bout
Of machine guns chattering . . .
And redoubled battering,
As if in fury at their daring ! . . .

No good staring.
Time soon now . . . home . . . house on a
    sunny hill . . .
Gone like a flickered page :
Time soon now . . . zero . . . will engage . . .

A sudden thrill—
" Fix bayonets ! "
Gods ! we have our fill
Of fear, hysteria, exultation, rage,
Rage to kill.

My heart burns hot, whiter and whiter,
Contracts tighter and tighter,
Until I stifle with the will
Long forged, now used
(Though utterly strained)—
O pounding heart,
Baffled, confused,
Heart panged, head singing, dizzily pained—
To do my part.

Blindness a moment. Sick.
There the men are !
Bayonets ready : click !
Time goes quick ;

A stumbled prayer . . . somehow a blazing star
In a blue night . . . where ?
Again prayer.
The tongue trips. Start :
How's time ? Soon now. Two minutes or less.
The gun's fury mounting higher . . .
Their utmost. I lift a silent hand. Unseen I bless
Those hearts will follow me.
And beautifully,
Now beautifully my will grips,
Soul calm and round and filmed and white !
A shout : " Men, no such order as retire ! "

I nod.
The whistle's 'twixt my lips . . .
I catch
A wan, worn smile at me.
Dear men !
The pale wrist-watch . . .
The quiet hand ticks on amid the din.
The guns again
Rise to a last fury, to a rage, a lust :
Kill ! Pound ! Kill ! Pound ! Pound !
Now comes the thrust !
My part . . . dizziness . . . will . . . but trust
These men. The great guns rise ;
Their fury seems to burst the earth and skies !

They lift.

Gather, heart, all thoughts that drift ;
Be steel, soul,

Compress thyself
Into a round, bright whole.
I cannot speak.

Time.   Time !

I hear my whistle shriek,
Between teeth set ;
I fling an arm up,
Scramble up the grime
Over the parapet !

I'm up.   Go on.
Something meets us.
Head down into the storm that greets us.

A wail.
Lights.   Blurr.
Gone.
On, on.   Lead.   Lĕăd.   Hail.
Spatter.   Whirr !   Whirr !
" *Toward that patch of brown ;*
Direction left."   Bullets a stream.
Devouring thought crying in a dream.
Men, crumpled, going down . . .
Go on.   Go.
Deafness.   Numbness.   The loudening tornado.
Bullets.   Mud.   Stumbling and skating.
My voice's strangled shout :
" *Steady pace, boys !* "
The still light : gladness.

" *Look, sir.   Look out !* "
Ha ! ha ! Bunched figures waiting.
Revolver levelled quick !
Flick !   Flick !
Red as blood.
Germans.   Germans.
Good !   O good !
Cool madness.   *Robert Nichols.*

6. WAR'S CATARACT

IN this red havoc of the patient earth,
      Though higher yet the tide of battle rise,
Now has the hero cast away disguise,
And out of ruin splendour comes to birth.
This is the field where Death and Honour meet,
And all the lesser company are low :
Pale Loveliness has left her mirror now
And walks the Court of Pain with silent feet.

From cliff to cliff war's cataract goes down,
Hurling its booming waters to the shock ;
And, tossing high their manes of gleaming spray,
The crested chargers leap from rock to rock,
While over all, dark though the thunder frown,
The rainbows climb above to meet the day.
                                    Herbert Asquith.

7. FULFILMENT

WAS there love once ?   I have forgotten her.
      Was there grief once ?   Grief yet is mine.
Other loves I have, men rough, but men who stir
More grief, more joy, than love of thee and thine.

Faces cheerful, full of whimsical mirth,
Lined by the wind, burned by the sun ;
Bodies enraptured by the abounding earth,
As whose children we are brethren : one.

And any moment may descend hot death
To shatter limbs ! pulp, tear, blast
Beloved soldiers who love rough life and breath
Not less for dying faithful to the last.

O the fading eyes, the grimed face turned bony,
Oped mouth gushing, fallen head,
Lessening pressure of a hand shrunk, clammed, and
    stony !
O sudden spasm, release of the dead !

Was there love once ?   I have forgotten her.
Was there grief once ?   Grief yet is mine.
O loved, living, dying, heroic soldier,
All, all, my joy, my grief, my love, are thine !
                                    Robert Nichols.

8. CHRIST IN FLANDERS

WE had forgotten You, or very nearly—
    You did not seem to touch us very nearly—
Of course we thought about You now and then ;
Especially in any time of trouble—
We knew that You were good in time of trouble—
    But we are very ordinary men.

And there were always other things to think of—
There's lots of things a man has got to think of—
    His work, his home, his pleasure, and his wife ;
And so we only thought of You on Sunday—
Sometimes, perhaps, not even on a Sunday—
    Because there's always lots to fill one's life.

And, all the while, in street or lane or byway—
In country lane, in city street, or byway—
    You walked among us, and we did not see.
Your feet were bleeding as You walked our pave-
        ments—
How *did* we miss Your footprints on our pavements ?—
    Can there be other folk as blind as we ?

Now we remember ; over here in Flanders—
(It isn't strange to think of You in Flanders)—
    This hideous warfare seems to make things clear.
We never thought about You much in England—
But now that we are far away from England,
    We have no doubts, we know that You are here.

You helped us pass the jest along the trenches—
Where, in cold blood, we waited in the trenches—
    You touched its ribaldry and made it fine.
You stood beside us in our pain and weakness—
We're glad to think You understand our weakness—
    Somehow it seems to help us not to whine.

We think about You kneeling in the Garden—
Ah ! God ! the agony of that dread Garden—
    We know You prayed for us upon the cross.

If anything could make us glad to bear it—
'Twould be the knowledge that You willed to bear it—
　　Pain—death—the uttermost of human loss.

Though we forgot You—You will not forget us—
We feel so sure that You will not forget us—
　　But stay with us until this dream is past.
And so we ask for courage, strength, and pardon—
Especially, I think, we ask for pardon—
　　And that You'll stand beside us to the last.
　　　　　　　　　　　　　Lucy Whitmell.

9. AT THE WARS

Now that I am ta'en away
　　And may not see another day
What is it to my eye appears ?
What sound rings in my stricken ears ?
Not even the voice of any friend
Or eyes beloved-world-without-end,
But scenes and sounds of the country-side
In far England across the tide :
An upland field when spring's begun,
Mellow beneath the evening sun. . . .
A circle of loose and lichened wall
Over which seven red pines fall. . . .
An orchard of wizen blossoming trees
Wherein the nesting chaffinches
Begin again the self-same song
All the late April day-time long. . .

Paths that lead a shelving course
Between the chalk scarp and the gorse
By English downs ; and oh ! too well
I hear the hidden, clanking bell
Of wandering sheep. . . . I see the brown
Twilight of the huge empty down. . . .
Soon blotted out ! for now a lane
Glitters with warmth of May-time rain,
And on a shooting briar I see
A yellow bird who sings to me.

O yellow-hammer, once I heard
Thy brief song when no other bird
Could to my sunk heart comfort bring ;
But now I would not have thee sing
So sharp thy note is with the pain
Of England I may not see again !
Yet sing thy song : there answereth
Deep in me a voice which saith :
  " The gorse upon the twilit down,
    The English loam so sunset brown,
    The bowed pines and the sheep-bells' clamour,
    The wet, lit lane and the yellow-hammer,
    The orchard and the chaffinch song
    Only to the Brave belong.
    And he shall lose their joy for aye
    If their price he cannot pay,
    Who shall find them dearer far
    Enriched by blood after long War."
                              Robert Nichols.

10. HOME THOUGHTS IN LAVENTIE

GREEN gardens in Laventie !
      Soldiers only know the street
Where the mud is churned and splashed about
      By battle-wending feet ;
And yet beside one stricken house there is a glimpse
    of grass.
      Look for it when you pass.

Beyond the church whose pitted spire
      Seems balanced on a strand
Of swaying stone and tottering brick
      Two roofless ruins stand,
And here behind the wreckage where the back wall
    should have been
      We found a garden green.

The grass was never trodden on,
      The little path of gravel
Was overgrown with celandine,
      No other folk did travel
Along its weedy surface, but the nimble-footed mouse
      Running from house to house.

So all among the vivid blades
      Of soft and tender grass
We lay, nor heard the limber wheels
      That pass and ever pass
In noisy continuity until their very rattle
      Seems in itself a battle.

At length we rose up from this ease
Of tranquil happy mind,
And searched the garden's little length
A fresh pleasaunce to find ;
And there some yellow daffodils and jasmine hanging
high
Did rest the tired eye.

The fairest and most fragrant
Of the many sweets we found,
Was a little bush of daphne flower
Upon a grassy mound,
And so thick were the blossoms set and so divine the
scent
That we were well content.

Hungry for spring, I bent my head,
The perfume fanned my face,
And all my soul was dancing
In that little lovely place,
Dancing with a measured step from wrecked and
shattered towns
Away upon the Downs.

I saw green banks of daffodil,
Slim poplars in the breeze,
Great tan-brown hares in gusty March
A-courting on the leas ;
And meadows with their glittering streams, and silver
scurrying dace,
Home—what a perfect place !

                    E. Wyndham Tennant.

11. BACK TO REST

A LEAPING wind from England,
　The skies without a stain,
Clean cut against the morning,
　Slim poplars after rain,
The foolish noise of sparrows
　And starlings in a wood—
After the grime of battle
　We know that these are good.

Death whining down from heaven,
　Death roaring from the ground,
Death stinking in the nostril,
　Death shrill in every sound,
Doubting we charged and conquered—
　Hopeless we struck and stood.
Now when the fight is ended
　We know that it was good.

We that have seen the strongest
　Cry like a beaten child,
The sanest eyes unholy,
　The cleanest hands defiled,
We that have known the heart-blood
　Less than the lees of wine,
We that have seen men broken,
　We know man is divine.

William Noel Hodgson.

12. OXFORD IN WAR-TIME

WHAT alters you, familiar lawn and tower,
    Arched alley, and garden green to the grey wall
With crumbling crevice and the old wine-red flower,
Solitary in summer sun ? for all

Is like a dream : I tread on dreams !   No stir
Of footsteps, voices, laughter !   Even the chime
Of many-memoried bells is lonelier
In this neglected ghostliness of Time.

What stealing touch of separation numb
Absents you ?   Yet my heart springs up to adore
The shrining of your soul, that is become
Nearer and oh ! far dearer than before.

It is as if I looked on the still face
Of a Mother, musing where she sits alone.
She is with her sons, she is not in this place ;
She is gone out into far lands unknown.

Because that filled horizon occupies
Her heart with mute prayer and divining fear,
Therefore her hands so calm lie, and her eyes
See nothing ; and men wonder at her here :

But far in France ; on the torn Flanders plain ;
By Sinai ; in the Macedonian snows ;
The fly-plagued sands of Tigris, heat and rain ;
On wandering water, where the black squall blows

Less danger than the bright wave ambushes,
She bears it out.   All the long day she bears,
And the sudden hour of instant challenges
To act, that searches all men, no man spares.

She is with her sons, leaving a virtue gone
Out of her sacred places : what she bred
Lives other life than this, that sits alone,
Though still in dream starrily visited !

For O in youth she lives, not in her age.
Her soul is with the springtime and the young ;
And she absents her from the learned page,
Studious of high histories yet unsung.

More passionately prized than wisdom's book
Because her own.   Her faith is in those eyes
That clear into the gape of hell can look,
Putting to proof ancient philosophies

Such as the virgin Muses would rehearse
Beside the silvery, swallow-haunted stream,
Under the grey towers.   But immortal verse
Is now exchanged for its immortal theme—

Victory ; proud loss ; and the enduring mind ;
Youth, that has passed all praises, and has won
More than renown, being that which faith divined
Reality more radiant than the sun.

She gave, she gives, more than all anchored days
Of dedicated lore, of storied art ;
And she resigns her beauty to men's gaze
To mask the riches of her bleeding heart.
Laurence Binyon.

13. THE NON-COMBATANT

AMONG a race high-handed, strong of heart,
  Sea-rovers, conquerors, builders in the waste,
He had his birth ; a nature too complete,
Eager and doubtful, no man's soldier sworn
And no man's chosen captain ; born to fail,
A name without an echo : yet he too
Within the cloister of his narrow days
Fulfilled the ancestral rites, and kept alive
The eternal fire ; it may be, not in vain ;
For out of those who dropped a downward glance
Upon the weakling huddled at his prayers,
Perchance some looked beyond him, and then first
Beheld the glory, and what shrine it filled,
And to what Spirit sacred : or perchance
Some heard him chanting, though but to himself,
The old heroic names : and went their way :
And hummed his music on the march to death.
Henry Newbolt.

14. EPITAPH ON AN ARMY OF MERCENARIES

THESE, in the day when Heaven was falling,
  The hour when Earth's foundation fled,
Followed their mercenary calling
  And took their wages and are dead.

Their shoulders held the sky suspended ;
  They stood, and Earth's foundations stay ;
What God abandoned, these defended
  And saved the sum of things for pay.

A. E. Housman.

15. THE VOLUNTEER

HERE lies the clerk who half his life had spent
    Toiling at ledgers in a city grey,
Thinking that so his days would drift away
With no lance broken in life's tournament :
Yet ever 'twixt the books and his bright eyes
The gleaming eagles of the legions came,
And horsemen, charging under phantom skies,
Went thundering past beneath the oriflamme

And now those waiting dreams are satisfied ;
From twilight to the halls of dawn he went ;
His lance is broken ; but he lies content
With that high hour, in which he lived and died.
And falling thus, he wants no recompense,
Who found his battle in the last resort;
Nor needs he any hearse to bear him hence,
Who goes to join the men of Agincourt.

Herbert Asquith.

16. THE WAR FILMS

O LIVING pictures of the dead,
    O songs without a sound,
O fellowship whose phantom tread
    Hallows a phantom ground—
How in a gleam have these revealed
    The faith we had not found.

We have sought God in a cloudy Heaven,
  We have passed by God on earth :
His seven sins and his sorrows seven,
  His wayworn mood and mirth,
Like a ragged cloak have hid from us
  The secret of his birth.

Brother of men, when now I see
  The lads go forth in line,
Thou knowest my heart is hungry in me
  As for thy bread and wine :
Thou knowest my heart is bowed in me
  To take their death for mine.

                 Henry Newbolt.

17. THE UNRETURNING SPRING

A LEAF on the grey sand-path
    Fallen, and fair with rime !
A yellow leaf, a scarlet leaf,
And a green leaf ere its time.

Days rolled in blood, days torn,
Days innocent, days burnt black,
What is it the wind is sighing
As the leaves float, swift or slack ?

The year's pale spectre is crying
For beauty invisibly shed,
For the things that never were told
And were killed in the minds of the dead.

                 Laurence Binyon.

18. HARROW AND FLANDERS

HERE in the marshland, past the battered bridge,
   One of a hundred grains untimely sown,
Here, with his comrades of the hard-won ridge,
     He rests, unknown.

His horoscope had seemed so plainly drawn—
   School triumphs earned apace in work and play ;
Friendships at will ; then love's delightful dawn
     And mellowing day ;

Home fostering hope ; some service to the State ;
   Benignant age ; then the long tryst to keep
Where in the yew-tree shadow congregate
     His fathers sleep.

Was here the one thing needful to distil
   From life's alembic, through this holier fate,
The man's essential soul, the hero will ?
     We ask ; and wait.

Lord Crewe.

19. IN MEMORIAM, A. H.

*(Auberon Herbert, Captain Lord Lucas, R.F.C., killed November 3rd
1916)*

THE wind had blown away the rain
   That all day long had soaked the level plain.
Against the horizon's fiery wrack,
The sheds loomed black.
And higher, in their tumultuous concourse met,
The streaming clouds, shot-riddled banners, wet

With the flickering storm,
Drifted and smouldered, warm
With flashes sent
From the lower firmament.
And they concealed—
They only here and there through rifts revealed
A hidden sanctuary of fire and light,
A city of chrysolite.

We looked and laughed and wondered, and I said :
That orange sea, those oriflammes outspread
Were like the fanciful imaginings
That the young painter flings
Upon the canvas bold,
Such as the sage and the old
Make mock at, saying it could never be ;
And you assented also, laughingly.
I wondered what they meant,
That flaming firmament,
Those clouds so grey so gold, so wet so warm,
So much of glory and so much of storm,
The end of the world, or the end
Of the war—remoter still to me and you, my friend.

Alas ! it meant not this, it meant not that :
It meant that now the last time you and I
Should look at the golden sky,
And the dark fields large and flat,
And smell the evening weather,
And laugh and talk and wonder both together.

The last, last time.   We nevermore should meet
In France or London street,
Or fields of home.   The desolated space
Of life shall nevermore
Be what it was before.
No one shall take your place.
No other face
Can fill that empty frame.
There is no answer when we call your name.
We cannot hear your step upon the stair.
We turn to speak and find a vacant chair.
Something is broken which we cannot mend.
God has done more than take away a friend
In taking you ; for all that we have left
Is bruised and irremediably bereft.
There is none like you.   Yet not that alone
Do we bemoan ;
But this ; that you were greater than the rest
And better than the best.
O liberal heart fast-rooted to the soil,
O lover of ancient freedom and proud toil,
Friend of the gipsies and all wandering song,
The forest's nursling and the favoured child
Of woodlands wild—
O brother to the birds and all things free,
Captain of liberty !

Deep in your heart the restless seed was sown ;
The vagrant spirit fretted in your feet ;
We wondered could you tarry long,
And brook for long the cramping street,

Or would you one day sail for shores unknown,
And shake from you the dust of towns, and spurn
The crowded market-place—and not return ?
You found a sterner guide ;
You heard the guns.   Then, to their distant fire,
Your dreams were laid aside ;
And on that day, you cast your heart's desire
Upon a burning pyre ;
You gave your service to the exalted need,
Until at last from bondage freed,
At liberty to serve as you loved best,
You chose the noblest way.   God did the rest.

So when the spring of the world shall shrive our stain,
After the winter of war,
When the poor world awakes to peace once more,
After such night of ravage and of rain,
You shall not come again.
You shall not come to taste the old spring weather,
To gallop through the soft untrampled heather,
To bathe and bake your body on the grass.
We shall be there, alas !
But not with you.   When Spring shall wake the earth,
And quicken the scarred fields to the new birth,
Our grief shall grow.   For what can Spring renew
More fiercely for us than the need of you ?

That night I dreamt they sent for me and said
That you were missing, " missing, missing—dead " :
I cried when in the morning I awoke,
And all the world seemed shrouded in a cloak ;

But when I saw the sun,
And knew another day had just begun,
I brushed the dream away, and quite forgot
The nightmare's ugly blot.
So was the dream forgot.   The dream came true.
Before the night I knew
That you had flown away into the air
For ever.   Then I cheated my despair.
I said
That you were safe—or wounded—but not dead.
Alas ! I knew
Which was the false and true.

And after days of watching, days of lead,
There came the certain news that you were dead.
You had died fighting, fighting against odds,
Such as in war the gods
Aethereal dared when all the world was young ;
Such fighting as blind Homer never sung,
Nor Hector nor Achilles never knew,
High in the empty blue.

High, high, above the clouds, against the setting sun,
The fight was fought, and your great task was done.

Of all your brave adventures this the last
The bravest was and best ;
Meet ending to a long embattled past,
This swift, triumphant, fatal quest,
Crowned with the wreath that never perisheth,
And diadem of honourable death ;

Swift Death aflame with offering supreme
And mighty sacrifice,
More than all mortal dream ;
A soaring death, and near to Heaven's gate ;
Beneath the very walls of Paradise.
Surely with soul elate,
You heard the destined bullet as you flew,
And surely your prophetic spirit knew
That you had well deserved that shining fate.

Here is no waste,
No burning Might-have-been,
No bitter after-taste,
None to censure, none to screen,
Nothing awry, nor anything misspent ;
Only content, content beyond content,
Which hath not any room for betterment.

God, Who had made you valiant, strong and swift,
And maimed you with a bullet long ago,
And cleft your riotous ardour with a rift,
And checked your youth's tumultuous overflow,
Gave back your youth to you,
And packed in moments rare and few
Achievements manifold
And happiness untold,
And bade you spring to Death as to a bride,
In manhood's ripeness, power and pride,
And on your sandals the strong wings of youth.

He let you leave a name
To shine on the entablatures of truth,
For ever :
To sound for ever in answering halls of fame.

For you soared onwards to that world which rags
Of clouds, like tattered flags,
Concealed ; you reached the walls of chrysolite,
The mansions white ;
And losing all, you gained the civic crown
Of that eternal town,
Wherein you passed a rightful citizen
Of the bright commonwealth ablaze beyond our ken.

Surely you found companions meet for you
In that high place ;
You met there face to face
Those you had never known, but whom you knew :
Knights of the Table Round,
And all the very brave, the very true,
With chivalry crowned ;
The captains rare,
Courteous and brave beyond our human air ;
Those who had loved and suffered overmuch,
Now free from the world's touch.
And with them were the friends of yesterday.
Who went before and pointed you the way ;
And in that place of freshness, light and rest,

Where Lancelot and Tristram vigil keep
Over their King's long sleep,

Surely they made a place for you,
Their long-expected guest,
Among the chosen few,
And welcomed you, their brother and their friend,
To that companionship which hath no end.

And in the portals of the sacred hall
You hear the trumpet's call,
At dawn upon the silvery battlement,
Re-echo through the deep
And bid the sons of God to rise from sleep,
And with a shout to hail
The sunrise on the city of the Grail :
The music that proud Lucifer in Hell
Missed more than all the joys that he forwent.
You hear the solemn bell
At vespers, when the oriflammes are furled ;
And then you know that somewhere in the world,
That shines far-off beneath you like a gem,
They think of you, and when you think of them
You know that they will wipe away their tears,
And cast aside their fears ;
That they will have it so,
And in no otherwise ;
That it is well with them because they know,
With faithful eyes,
Fixed forward and turned upwards to the skies,
That it is well with you,
Among the chosen few,
Among the very brave, the very true.

                              Maurice Baring.

20. LAMENT

WE who are left, how shall we look again
  Happily on the sun or feel the rain
Without remembering how they who went
Ungrudgingly and spent
Their lives for us loved, too, the sun and rain ?

A bird among the rain-wet lilac sings—
But we, how shall we turn to little things
And listen to the birds and winds and streams
Made holy by their dreams,
Nor feel the heart-break in the heart of things ?

Wilfrid Wilson Gibson.

21. THE DYING PATRIOT

DAY breaks on England down the Kentish hills,
  Singing in the silence of the meadow-footing rills,
Day of my dreams, O day !
  I saw them march from Dover, long ago,
  With a silver cross before them, singing low,
Monks of Rome from their home where the blue seas
      break in foam,
  Augustine with his feet of snow.

Noon strikes on England, noon on Oxford town,
—Beauty she was statue cold—there's blood upon her
      gown :
Noon of my dreams, O noon !
  Proud and godly kings had built her, long ago,
  With her towers and tombs and statues all arow,
With her fair and floral air and the love that lingers
      there,
  And the streets where the great men go.

Evening on the olden, the golden sea of Wales,
When the first star shivers and the last wave pales :
O evening dreams !
   There's a house that Britons walked in, long ago,
   Where now the springs of ocean fall and flow,
And the dead robed in red and sea-lilies overhead
   Sway when the long winds blow.

Sleep not, my country : though night is here, afar
Your children of the morning are clamorous for war :
Fire in the night, O dreams !
   Though she send you as she sent you, long ago,
   South to desert, east to ocean, west to snow,
West of these out to seas colder than the Hebrides
         I must go
   Where the fleet of stars is anchored and the young
         Star-captains glow.
                                        J. E. Flecker.

22. MEN WHO MARCH AWAY

(Song of the Soldiers)

WHAT of the faith and fire within us
      Men who march away
   Ere the barn-cocks say
   Night is growing gray,
Leaving all that here can win us ;
What of the faith and fire within us
   Men who march away ?

Is it a purblind prank, O think you,
    Friend with the musing eye,
    Who watch us stepping by
    With doubt and dolorous sigh ?
Can much pondering so hoodwink you !
Is it a purblind prank, O think you,
    Friend with the musing eye ?

Nay.   We well see what we are doing,
    Though some may not see—
    Dalliers as they be—
    England's need are we ;
Her distress would leave us rueing :
Nay.   We'll see what we are doing,
    Though some may not see.

In our heart of hearts believing
    Victory crowns the just,
    And that braggarts must
    Surely bite the dust,
Press we to the field ungrieving,
In our heart of hearts believing
    Victory crowns the just.

Hence the faith and fire within us
    Men who march away
    Ere the barn-cocks say
    Night is growing gray,
Leaving all that here can win us ;
Hence the faith and fire within us
    Men who march away.

                              Thomas Hardy

September 5, 1914.

    P.T.D. 2—2

23. ON BEHALF OF SOME IRISHMEN NOT FOLLOWERS OF TRADITION

THEY call us aliens, we are told,
  Because our wayward visions stray
From that dim banner they unfold,
The dreams of worn-out yesterday.
The sum of all the past is theirs,
The creeds, the deeds, the fame, the name,
Whose death-created glory flares
And dims the spark of living flame.
They weave the necromancer's spell,
And burst the graves where martyrs slept,
Their ancient story to retell,
Renewing tears the dead have wept.
And they would have us join their dirge,
This worship of an extinct fire
In which they drift beyond the verge
Where races all outworn expire.
The worship of the dead is not
A worship that our hearts allow,
Though every famous shade were wrought
With woven thorns above the brow.

We fling our answer back in scorn :
" We are less children of this clime
Than of some nation yet unborn
Or empire in the womb of time.
We hold the Ireland in the heart
More than the land our eyes have seen,
And love the goal for which we start
More than the tale of what has been."

The generations as they rise
May live the life men lived before,
Still hold the thought once held as wise,
Go in and out by the same door.
We leave the easy peace it brings :
The few we are shall still unite
In fealty to unseen kings
Or unimaginable light.
We would no Irish sign efface,
But yet our lips would gladlier hail
The firstborn of the Coming Race
Than the last splendour of the Gael.
No blazoned banner we unfold—
One charge alone we give to youth,
Against the sceptred myth to hold
The golden heresy of truth.

A. E.

24. I VOW TO THEE, MY COUNTRY

(Written January 12th, 1918, the last night which he spent at the British Embassy at Washington, at the end of his service to England, and hardly more than a month before his death.)

I vow to thee, my country—all earthly things
      above—
Entire and whole and perfect, the service of my love,
The love that asks no questions : the love that stands
      the test,
That lays upon the altar the dearest and the best :
The love that never falters, the love that pays the
      price,
The love that makes undaunted the final sacrifice.

And there's another country, I've heard of long ago—
Most dear to them that love her, most great to them
    that know—
We may not count her armies : we may not see her
    king—
Her fortress is a faithful heart, her pride is suffering—
And soul by soul and silently her shining bounds
    increase,
And her ways are ways of gentleness and all her paths
    are peace.

Cecil Spring-Rice.

25. HAPPY IS ENGLAND NOW

THERE is not anything more wonderful
    Than a great people moving towards the deep
Of an unguessed and unfeared future ; nor
Is aught so dear of all held dear before
As the new passion stirring in their veins
When the destroying Dragon wakes from sleep.

Happy is England now, as never yet !
And though the sorrows of the slow days fret
Her faithfullest children, grief itself is proud.
Ev'n the warm beauty of this spring and summer
That turns to bitterness turns then to gladness,
Since for this England the beloved ones died.

Happy is England in the brave that die
For wrongs not hers and wrongs so sternly hers ;

Happy in those that give, give, and endure
The pain that never the new years may cure ;
Happy in all her dark woods, green fields, towns,
Her hills and rivers and her chafing sea.

Whate'er was dear before is dearer now.
There's not a bird singing upon his bough
But sings the sweeter in our English ears :
There's not a nobleness of heart, hand, brain
But shines the purer ; happiest is England now
In those that fight, and watch with pride and tears.

John Freeman.

26. AVE, MATER—ATQUE VALE

THE deathless mother, grey and battle-scarred,
    Lies in the sanctuary of stately trees,
Where the deep Northern night is saffron starred
    Above her head, and thro' the dusk she sees
God's shadowy fortress keep unsleeping guard.

From her full breast we drank of joy and mirth
    And gave to her a boy's unreasoned heart,
Wherein Time's fullness was to bring to birth
    Such passionate allegiance that to part
Seemed like the passing of all light on earth.

Now on the threshold of a man's estate,
    With a new depth of love akin to pain
I ask thy blessing, while I dedicate
    My life and sword, with promise to maintain
Thine ancient honour yet inviolate.

Last night dream-hearted in the Abbey's spell
    We stood to sing old Simeon's passing hymn,
When sudden splendour of the sunset fell
    Full on my eyes, and passed and left all dim—
At once a summons and a deep farewell.

I am content—our life is but a trust
    From the great hand of God, and if I keep
The immortal Treasure clean of mortal rust
    Against His claim, 'tis well, and let me sleep
Among the not dishonourable dust.

William Noel Hodgson.

27. THE SCRIBE

WHAT lovely things
        Thy hand hath made :
The smooth-plumed bird
In its emerald shade,
The seed of the grass,
The speck of stone
Which the wayfaring ant
Stirs—and hastes on !

Though I should sit
By some tarn in thy hills,
Using its ink
As the spirit wills
To write of Earth's wonders,
Its live, willed things,
Flit would the ages
On soundless wings

Ere unto Z
My pen drew nigh ;
Leviathan told,
And the honey-fly :
And still would remain
My wit to try—
My worn reeds broken,
The dark tarn dry,
All words forgotten—
Thou, Lord, and I.

Walter de la Mare.

28. WIND'S WORK

KATE rose up early as fresh as a lark,
   Almost in time to see vanish the dark ;
Jack rather later, bouncing from bed,
Saw fade on the dawn's cheek the last flush of red ;
Yet who knows
When the wind rose ?

Kate went to watch the new lambs at their play
And stroke the white calf born yesterday ;
Jack sought the woods where trees grow tall
As who would learn to swarm them all :
Yet who knows
Where the wind goes ?

Kate has sown candy-tuft, lupins and peas,
Carnations, forget-me-not and heart's ease ;

Jack has sown cherry-pie, marigold,
Love-that-lies-bleeding and snap-dragons bold :
But who knows
What the wind sows ?

Kate knows a thing or two useful at home,
Darns like a fairy, and churns like a gnome ;
Jack is a wise man at shaping a stick,
Once he's in the saddle the pony may kick.
But hark to the wind how it blows !
None comes, none goes,
None reaps or mows,
No friends turn foes,
No hedge bears sloes,
And no cock crows,
But the wind knows !

T. Sturge Moore.

29. THE LAMP FLOWER

THE campion white
    Above the grass
Her lamps doth light
    Where fairies pass.

Softly they show
    The secret way,
Unflickering glow
    For elf and fay.

My little thought
    Hath donned her shoe,
And all untaught
    Gone dancing too.

Sadly I peer
　Among the grass
And seem to hear
　The fairies pass,

But where they go
　I cannot see,
Too faintly glow
　The lamps for me.

My thought is gone
　With fay and elf,
We mope alone,
　I and myself.

Margaret Cecilia Furse.

30. JULY FUGITIVE

CAN you tell me where has hid her,
　Pretty Maid July ?
I would swear one day ago
　She passed by,
I would swear that I do know
The blue bliss of her eye :
" Tarry, maid, maid," I bid her ;
　But she hastened by.
Do you know where she has hid her,
　Maid July ?

Yet in truth it needs must be
　The flight of her is old ;
Yet in truth it needs must be,
　For her nest, the earth, is cold.

P.T.D. 2—2*

No more in the poolèd Even
 Wade her rosy feet,
Dawn-flakes no more plash from them
 To poppies 'mid the wheat.

She has muddied the day's oozes
 With her petulant feet ;
Scared the clouds that floated
 As sea-birds they were,
Slow on the cœrule
 Lulls of the air,
Lulled on the luminous
 Levels of air :
She has chidden in a pet
 All her stars from her ;
Now they wander loose and sigh
 Through the turbid blue,
Now they wander, weep, and cry—
 Yea, and I too—
" Where are you, sweet July,
 Where are you ? "

Who hath beheld her footprints,
 Or the pathway she goes ?
Tell me, wind, tell me, wheat,
 Which of you knows ?
Sleeps she swathed in the flushed Arctic
 Night of the rose ?
Or lie her limbs like Alp-glow
 On the lily's snows ?

Gales, that are all-visitant,
　　Find the runaway ;
And for him who findeth her
　　(I do charge you say)
I will throw largesse of broom
　　Of this summer's mintage,
I will broach a honey-bag
　　Of the bee's best vintage.
Breezes, wheat, flowers sweet,
　　None of them knows !
How then shall we lure her back
　　From the way she goes ?
For it were a shameful thing,
　　Saw we not this comer
Ere Autumn camp upon the fields
　　Red with rout of Summer.

When the bird quits the cage,
　　We set the cage outside,
With seed and with water,
　　And the door wide,
Haply we may win it so
　　Back to abide.
Hang her cage of earth out
　　O'er Heaven's sunward wall,
Its four gates open, winds in watch
　　By reinèd cars at all ;
Relume in hanging hedgerows
　　The rain-quenched blossom
And roses sob their tears out
　　On the gale's warm heaving bosom ;

Shake the lilies till their scent
    Over-drip their rims,
That our runaway may see
    We do know her whims :
Sleek the tumbled waters out
    For her travelled limbs ;
Strew and smooth blue night thereon,
    There will—O not doubt her !—
The lovely sleepy lady lie,
    With all her stars about her !

Francis Thompson.

31. SEPTEMBER

SPRING is past and over these many days,
    Spring and summer. The leaves of September
        droop,
Yellowing and all but dead on the patient trees.
Nor is there any hope in me.   I walk
Slowly homeward.   Night is as empty and dark
Behind my eyes as it is dark without
And empty round about me and over me.
But, looking up, suddenly I see
Leaves in the upthrown light of a street lamp shine
Clear and luminous, young and so transparent,
They seem but the coloured foam of air, green fire,
No more than the scarce embodied thoughts of leaves ;
And it is spring within that circle of light.
Oh, magical brightness !—the old leaves are made new.
In the mind, too, some coloured accident
Of beauty revives and makes all young again.
A chance light meaningless shines and it is Spring.

Aldous Huxley.

32. TEMPER IN OCTOBER

HE rode at furious speed to Broken Edge,
And he was very angry, very small ;
But God was kind, knowing he needed not
A scolding, nor a swift unpleasant fall,
Nor any high reproach of soul at all.
" It matters not," said Reason and Good Sense ;
" Absurd to let a trifle grow immense."
" It matters very much," said Busy Brain ;
" You cannot be content and calm again,
For you are angry in a righteous cause."
" Poor, queer old Waxy ! " laughed the hips and haws.
" God has a sense of humour," said a ball
Of orange-gold inside a spindle-berry—
" And ' Christ our Lorde is full exceeding merrie.' "

He lingered in the lane at Broken Edge,
Bryony berries burned from every hedge ;
Snails in the deep wet grass of fairy rings
Told him of unimaginable things.
Love was in all the colours of the sky,
Love in the folded shadows of the high
Blue hills, as quiet as any Easter Eve.
(O fool, O blind and earthbound thus to grieve !)

He turned his horse.   Through level sunset-gleams
He saw a sudden little road that curled
And climbed elusive to a sky of dreams.
His anger over Broken Edge was hurled
To scatter into nothing on a gust
Of wind which brought the twilight to the trees.

The drifted leaves, the white October dust
Hiding the beechnuts for the squirrels' store,
Heard the low whisper spoken on his knees :—
" God, You have made a very perfect world,
Don't let me spoil it ever any more."

V. L. Edminson.

33. TO IRON FOUNDERS AND OTHERS

WHEN you destroy a blade of grass
　　　You poison England at her roots :
Remember no man's foot can pass
Where evermore no green life shoots.

You force the birds to wing too high
Where your unnatural vapours creep :
Surely the living rocks shall die
When birds no rightful distance keep.

You have brought down the firmament
And yet no heaven is more near ;
You shape huge deeds without event,
And half-made men believe and fear.

Your worship is your furnaces,
Which, like old idols, lost obscenes,
Have molten bowels ; your vision is
Machines for making more machines.

O, you are busied in the night,
Preparing destinies of rust ;
Iron misused must turn to blight
And dwindle to a tetter'd crust.

The grass, forerunner of life, has gone,
But plants that spring in ruins and shards
Attend until your dream is done :
I have seen hemlock in your yards.

The generations of the worm
Know not your loads piled on their soil ;
Their knotted ganglions shall wax firm
Till your strong flagstones heave and toil.

When the old hollow'd earth is crack'd,
And when, to grasp more power and feasts,
Its ores are emptied, wasted, lack'd,
The middens of your burning beasts

Shall be raked over till they yield
Last priceless slags for fashionings high,
Ploughs to wake grass in every field,
Chisels men's hands to magnify.

Gordon Bottomley.

34. DUCKS

I

FROM troubles of the world
   I turn to ducks,
Beautiful comical things
Sleeping or curled
Their heads beneath white wings
By water cool,
Or finding curious things
To eat in various mucks
Beneath the pool,

Tails uppermost, or waddling
Sailor-like on the shores
Of ponds, or paddling
—Left! right!—with fanlike feet
Which are for steady oars
When they (white galleys) float
Each bird a boat
Rippling at will the sweet
Wide waterway . . .
When night is fallen *you* creep
Upstairs, but drakes and dillies
Nest with pale water-stars,
Moonbeams and shadow bars,
And water-lilies:
Fearful too much to sleep
Since they've no locks
To click against the teeth
Of weasel and fox.
And warm beneath
Are eggs of cloudy green
Whence hungry rats and lean
Would stealthily suck
New life, but for the mien,
The bold ferocious mien
Of the mother-duck.

II

Yes, ducks are valiant things
On nests of twigs and straws,
And ducks are soothy things
And lovely on the lake

When that the sunlight draws
Thereon their pictures dim
In colours cool.
And when beneath the pool
They dabble, and when they swim
And make their rippling rings,
O ducks are beautiful things!

But ducks are comical things :—
As comical as you.
Quack!
They waddle round, they do.
They eat all sorts of things,
And then they quack.
By barn and stable and stack
They wander at their will,
But if you go too near
They look at you through black
Small topaz-tinted eyes
And wish you ill.
Triangular and clear
They leave their curious track
In mud at the water's edge,
And there amid the sedge
And slime they gobble and peer
Saying " Quack! quack!"

III

When God had finished the stars and whirl of coloured
    suns
He turned His mind from big things to fashion little
    ones,

Beautiful tiny things (like daisies) He made, and then
He made the comical ones in case the minds of men
      Should stiffen and become
      Dull, humourless and glum :
And so forgetful of their Maker be
As to take even themselves—*quite seriously.*
Caterpillars and cats are lively and excellent puns :
All God's jokes are good—even the practical ones !
And as for the duck, I think God must have smiled
    a bit
Seeing those bright eyes blink on the day He fashioned
    it.
And He's probably laughing still at the sound that
    came out of its bill !

                      F. W. Harvey.

35. EVERYONE SANG

EVERYONE suddenly burst out singing ;
    And I was filled with such delight
As prisoned birds must find in freedom
Winging wildly across the white
Orchards and dark green fields ; on ; on ; and out of
    sight.

Everyone's voice was suddenly lifted,
And beauty came like the setting sun.
My heart was shaken with tears, and horror
Drifted away. . . . O, but every one
Was a bird ; and the song was wordless ; the singing
    will never be done.

                    Siegfried Sassoon.

36. THE WAGGONER

THE old waggon drudges through the miry lane
 By the skulking pond where the pollards frown,
Notched, dumb, surly images of pain ;
 On a dulled earth the night droops down.

Wincing to slow and wistful airs
 The leaves on the shrubbed oaks know their hour,
And the unknown wandering spoiler bares
 The thorned black hedge of a mournful shower.

Small bodies fluster in the dead brown wrack
 As the stumbling shaft-horse jingles past,
And the waggoner flicks his whip a crack :
 The odd light flares on shadows vast

Over the lodges and oasts and byres
 Of the darkened farm ; the moment hangs wan
As though nature flagged and all desires.
 But in the dim court the ghost is gone

From the hug-secret yew to the penthouse wall,
 And stooping there seems to listen to
The waggoner leading the gray to stall,
 As centuries past itself would do.

Edmund Blunden.

37. MOONLIT APPLES

AT the top of the house the apples are laid in rows,
 And the skylight lets the moonlight in, and those
Apples are deep-sea apples of green. There goes
 A cloud on the moon in the autumn night.

A mouse in the wainscot scratches, and scratches, and
    then
There is no sound at the top of the house of men
Or mice ; and the cloud is blown, and the moon again
    Dapples the apples with deep-sea light.

They are lying in rows there, under the gloomy beams ;
On the sagging floor ; they gather the silver streams
Out of the moon, those moonlit apples of dreams,
    And quiet is the steep stair under.

In the corridors under there is nothing but sleep.
And stiller than ever on orchard boughs they keep
Tryst with the moon, and deep is the silence, deep
    On moon-washed apples of wonder.

                                        John Drinkwater.

38. MEMORY

IN silence and in darkness memory wakes
    Her million sheathèd buds and breaks
That day-long winter when the light and noise
And hard bleak breath of the outward-looking will
Made barren her tender soil, when every voice
Of her million airy birds was muffled or still.

One bud-sheath breaks :
One sudden voice awakes.
What change grew in our hearts seeing one night
That moth-winged ship drifting across the bay,
Her broad sail dimly white
On cloudy waters and hills as vague as they ?

Some new thing touched our spirit with distant
     delight,
Half-seen, half-noticed, as we loitered down,
Talking in whispers, to the little town,
     Down from the narrow hill
     Talking in whispers, for the air so still
Imposed its stillness on our lips and made
A quiet equal with the equal shade
That filled the slanting walk.   That phantom now
Slides with slack canvas and unwhispering prow
Through the dark sea that this dark room has made.
Or the night of the closed eyes will turn to-day
And all day's colours start out of the gray.
The sun burns on the water.   The tall hills
Push up their shady groves into the sky
And fail and cease where the intense light spills
Its parching torrent on the gaunt and dry
Rock of the further mountains, whence the snow
That softened their harsh edges long is gone.
     And nothing tempers now
The hot flood falling on the barren stone.

     O memory, take and keep
All that my eyes, your servants, bring you home—
Those other days beneath the low white dome
     Of smooth-spread clouds that creep
     As slow and soft as sleep,
When shade grows pale and the cypress stands upright,
     Distinct in the cool light,
Rigid and solid as a dark, hewn stone ;
     And many another night

That melts in darkness on the narrow quays
And changes every colour and every tone
And soothes the waters to a softer ease,
When under constellations coldly bright
The homeward sailors sing their way to bed
On ships that motionless in harbour float.
The circling harbour lights flash green and red ;
And, out beyond, a steady travelling boat
Breaking the swell with slow industrious oars
    At each stroke pours
Pale lighted water from the lifted blade.
Now in the painted houses all around
    Slow darkening windows call
The empty unwatched middle of the night.
The tide's few inches rise without a sound.
On the black promontory's windless head,
The last awake, the fireflies rise and fall
And tangle up their dithering skeins of light.

    O memory, take and keep
All that my eyes, your servants, bring you home !
    Thick through the changing year
The unexpected, rich-charged moments come,
    That you 'twixt wake and sleep
In the lids of the closed eyes shall make appear.
    This is life's certain good,
Though in the end it be not good at all
    When the dark end arises
And the stripped, startled spirit must let fall
    The amulets that could
Prevail with life's but not death's sad devices.

Then, like a child from whom an older child
Forces its gathered treasures,
Its beads and shells and strings of withered flowers,
    Tokens of recent pleasures,
The soul must lose in eyes weeping and wild
    Those prints of vanished hours.

Edward Shanks.

39. EVENING OVER THE FOREST

WATCH.
    What is it you see ?

The stark bough of an oak.
Beyond it the evening sky.
Clear, clear the evening sky
And green like a green pearl.

Did you hear ?
What did you hear ?

The harsh cry of a bird,
Beyond it the evening sky.
Still, still the evening sky
And green like a green pearl.

Oh, search.
What is it you see ?

Fiery snowy little cloud
Sailing to sleep in the sky.

Dim, dim the evening sky
Like a deep green pearl.

Come away.
Come away.

Beatrice Mayor.

40. THE LATE, LAST ROOK

THE old gilt vane and spire receive
    The last beam eastward striking ;
The first shy bat to peep at eve
Has found her to his liking.
The western heaven is dull and grey,
The last red glow has followed day.

The late, last rook is housed and will
With cronies lie till morrow ;
If there's a rook loquacious still
In dream he hunts a furrow,
And flaps behind a spectre team,
Or ghostly scarecrows walk his dream.

Ralph Hodgson.

41. THE SUNKEN GARDEN

SPEAK not—whisper not ;
    Here bloweth thyme and bergamot ;
Softly on the evening hour
Secret herbs their spices shower,

Dark-spiked rosemary and myrrh,
Lean-stalked, purple lavender ;
Hides within her bosom, too,
All her sorrows, bitter rue.

Breathe not—trespass not ;
Of this green and darkling spot,
Latticed from the moon's beams,
Perchance a distant dreamer dreams ;
Perchance upon its darkening air,
The unseen ghosts of children fare,
Faintly swinging, sway and sweep,
Like lovely sea-flowers in its deep ;
While, unmoved, to watch and ward,
'Mid its gloomed and daisied sward,
Stands with bowed and dewy head
That one little leaden lad.

Walter de la Mare.

42. MY GARDEN

A GARDEN is a lovesome thing, God wot !
   Rose plot,
 Fringed pool,
Ferned grot—
  The veriest school
  Of peace ; and yet the fool
Contends that God is not—
Not God ! in gardens ! when the eve is cool ?
  Nay, but I have a sign ;
  'Tis very sure God walks in mine.

T. E. Brown.

43. THE DESERTED GARDEN
Ypres, July 1917

I LOVE this garden, for you used to play
　About its haunted shadows long ago :
The years glide by in waves of blossom gay,
　And tides of jewelled snow.

Each summer brings the drowsy bees that doze
　Among the lazy flowers till you return :
Around your arbour the clematis grows,
　And red carnations burn.

Your spirit ever haunts my memory,
　As some faint echo when the hour is late :
The tall white hollyhocks wait dreamily
　Beside the crooked gate.

The jessamine that twinkles in the light,
　Still watches idly through the window-pane :
While scented stocks do weave their spell each night,
　In case you come again.

The silent trees remember, for they cast
　Their form just where your footsteps seem to lag :
The honeysuckle spreads its trailers fast,
　And the old palings sag.

Nor do the pensive columbines forget,
　Because they still unfold their little flowers :
The fragrance of devotion lingers yet
　Across the listless hours.

There is no stir ; the eager moments fly,
 Breathless as embers dwindling in the gloom :
No leaf dare fall ; the shadows loiter by,
 Like gnomes about my room.

Above the lattice where the roses cling,
 The fire-flies dart as they did long ago :
My heart would break if any bird should sing,
 Or if the wind should blow.

Alasdair Alpin MacGregor.

44. A DESERTED HOME

HERE where the fields lie lonely and untended,
 Once stood the old house grey among the trees,
Once to the hills rolled the waves of the cornland—
 Long waves and golden, softer than the sea's.

Long, long ago has the ploughshare rusted,
 Long has the barn stood roofless and forlorn ;
But oh ! far away are some who still remember
 The songs of the young girls binding up the corn.

Here where the windows shone across the darkness,
 Here where the stars once watched above the fold,
Still watch the stars, but the sheepfold is empty ;
 Falls now the rain where the hearth glowed of old.

Here where the leagues of melancholy lough-sedge
 Moan in the wind round the grey forsaken shore,
Once waved the corn in the mid-month of autumn,
 Once sped the dance when the corn was on the floor.

Sidney Royse Lysaght.

45. THE BARN

RAIN-SUNKEN roof, grown green and thin
　　For sparrows' nests and starlings' nests ;
Dishevelled eaves ; unwieldy doors,
Cracked rusty pump, and oaken floors,
And idly-pencilled names and jests
　　Upon the posts within.

The light pales at the spider's lust,
The wind tangs through the shattered pane :
An empty hop-poke spreads across
The gaping frame to mend the loss
And keeps out sun as well as rain,
　　Mildewed with clammy dust.

The smell of apples stored in hay
And homely cattle-cake is there.
Use and disuse have come to terms,
The walls are hollowed out by worms,
But men's feet keep the mid-floor bare
　　And free from worse decay.

All merry noise of hens astir
Or sparrows squabbling on the roof
Comes to the barn's broad open door ;
You hear upon the stable floor
Old hungry Dapple strike his hoof,
　　And the blue fan-tail's whir.

The barn is old, and very old,
But not a place of spectral fear.
Cobwebs and dust and speckling sun
Come to old buildings every one.
Long since they made their dwelling here,
 And here you may behold

Nothing but simple wane and change ;
Your tread will wake no ghost, your voice
Will fall on silence undeterred.
No phantom wailing will be heard,
Only the farm's blithe cheerful noise ;
 The barn is old, not strange.

      Edmund Blunden.

46. ROADS

I LOVE roads :
 The goddesses that dwell
Far along invisible
Are my favourite gods.

Roads go on
While we forget, and are
Forgotten like a star
That shoots and is gone.

On this earth 'tis sure
We men have not made
Anything that doth fade
So soon, so long endure :

The hill road wet with rain
In the sun would not gleam
Like a winding stream
If we trod it not again.

They are lonely
While we sleep, lonelier
For lack of the traveller
Who is now a dream only.

From dawn's twilight
And all the clouds like sheep
On the mountains of sleep
They wind into the night.

The next turn may reveal
Heaven : upon the crest
The close pine clump, at rest
And black, may Hell conceal.

Often footsore, never
Yet of the road I weary,
Though long and steep and dreary,
As it winds on for ever.

Helen of the roads,
The mountain ways of Wales
And the Mabinogion tales
Is one of the true gods,

Abiding in the trees,
The threes and fours so wise,
The larger companies,
That by the roadside be,

And beneath the rafter
Else uninhabited
Excepting by the dead ;
And it is her laughter

At morn and night I hear
When the thrush cock sings
Bright irrelevant things,
And when the chanticleer

Calls back to their own night
Troops that make loneliness
With their light footsteps' press,
As Helen's own are light.

Now all roads lead to France
And heavy is the tread
Of the living ; but the dead
Returning lightly dance :

Whatever the road bring
To me or take from me,
They keep me company
With their pattering,

Crowding the solitude
Of the loops over the downs,
Hushing the roar of towns
And their brief multitude.

Edward Thomas.

47. THE HOMECOMING OF THE SHEEP

THE sheep are coming home in Greece,
  Hark the bells on every hill !
Flock by flock, and fleece by fleece,
Wandering wide a little piece
Thro' the evening red and still,
Stopping where the pathways cease,
Cropping with a hurried will.

Thro' the cotton-bushes low
Merry boys with shouldered crooks
Close in a single row,
Shout among them as they go
With one bell-ring o'er the brooks.
Such delight you never know
Reading it from gilded books.

Before the early stars are bright
Cormorants and sea-gulls call,
And the moon comes large and white
Filling with a lovely light
The ferny curtained waterfall.
Then sleep wraps every bell up tight
And the climbing moon grows small.

Francis Ledwidge.

48. OUT IN THE DARK

OUT in the dark over the snow
　　The fallow fawns invisible go
With the fallow doe ;
And the winds blow
Fast as the stars are slow.

Stealthily the dark haunts round
And, when a lamp goes, without sound
At a swifter bound
Than the swiftest hound,
Arrives, and all else is drowned ;

And I and star and wind and deer
Are in the dark together—near,
Yet far,—and fear
Drums in my ear
In that sage company drear.

How weak and little is the light,
All the universe of sight,
Love and delight,
Before the might,
If you love it not, of night.
Edward Thomas.

49. DRIVING SHEEP

THE green east flows with the tides of the rose
　　Between the bars of night, half-drawn.
The moon shines cold and faint on the fold
　　Where sheep glimmer, gray in the dawn.

Oh, thin like a dream their sad cries seem,
  Caught high above time and space ;
And old as the world, from out fleece dew-pearled,
  Gazes each meek sheep-face.
Dazed with sleep, and numb, the sheep-women come,
  And open the field gate wide.
The sheep surge out in an idiot rout,
  Like gray foam swept on a tide.
Keep steady, move slow, we've three miles to go
  To Grantchester from Chalk Field pen.
Herd them up all the way, lest some go astray,
  Of our imbecile two score and ten.
Unreasoning, blind, each poor unhinged mind
  Takes its thought from the sheep next ahead.
Through each hedge gate (if you reach it too late)
  They charge, wild and pale, like the dead.
Their lilting bleat, their sharp, scuttling feet,
  Are strange, strange as dreams before day,
And . . . counting the sheep . . . we sway . . . into
    sleep . . .
  And trail along . . . foolish as they.

The wide tides of gold surge, quiet and cold ;
  The green west turns deep blue ;
The moon's worn slip very soon will dip,
  Like a pale night-bird, from view.
There seems no sound in the world all round
  But of horn feet and quavering cries
In the young, cold hour . . . Like flame, like a flower,
  The sun springs, huge with surprise.

                                    Rose Macaulay.

50. THE DOWNS

O BOLD majestic downs, smooth, fair and lonely;
   O still solitude, only matched in the skies;
    Perilous in steep places,
    Soft in the level races,
Where sweeping in phantom silence the cloudland flies;
With lovely undulation of fall and rise;
    Entrenched with thickets thorned,
By delicate miniature dainty flowers adorned !

I climb your crown, and lo ! a sight surprising
Of sea in front uprising, steep and wide :
    And scattered ships ascending
    To heaven, lost in the blending
Of distant blues, where water and sky divide,
Urging their engines against wind and tide,
    And all so small and slow
They seem to be wearily pointing the way they would
      go.

The accumulated murmur of soft plashing,
Of waves on rocks dashing and searching the sands,
    Takes my ear, in the veering
    Baffled wind, as rearing
Upright at the cliff, to the gullies and rifts he stands;
And his conquering surges scour out over the lands;
    While again at the foot of the downs
He masses his strength to recover the topmost crowns.

Robert Bridges.

51. THE DOWNS

OH ! the downs high to the cool sky ;
      And the feel of the sun-warmed moss ;
And each cardoon, like a full moon,
Fairy-spun of the thistle floss ;
And the beech grove, and a wood dove,
And the trail where the shepherds pass ;
And the lark's song, and the wind song,
And the scent of the parching grass !

John Galsworthy

52. SHEPHERD APOLLO

CLIMB with me, Laomedon's white fleeces,
      Upward to the hilltops, up to Ida,
To unshaded dews and earliest dawning.
Young and lustrous, god and yet a servant,
As a star past rock and tree I climb.
Raise your heads erect, ye flocks, and listen
To the note I strike from off my lyre !
They have heard, they stand each head erected ;
Thus they wait the Grazing-Tune that woos
Slowly to the ridges and the sky.
I have struck it : all submissive listen,
Till they feed in mystery, advancing,
Drawn to solemn paces by a spell ;
Then to sharper strains one way they hurry,
Fleece by fleece around me, till I strike
Sweet, soft notes that lay them down to slumber,
I beside them, where the sun no more
Falls across us, but the chilling moonlight :

There we sleep, my flock and I together,
I, a god, though servant of a king.

Michael Field.

53. SONG OF POPLARS

SHEPHERD, to yon tall poplars tune your flute :
    Let them pierce keenly, subtly shrill,
The slow blue rumour of the hill ;
Let the grass cry with an anguish of evening gold,
And the great sky be mute.

Then hearken how the poplar trees unfold
Their buds, yet close and gummed and blind,
In airy leafage of the mind,
Rustling in silvery whispers the twin-hued scales
That fade not nor grow old.

" Poplars and fountains and you cypress spires
Springing in dark and rusty flame,
Seek you aught that hath a name ?
Or say, say : Are you all an upward agony
Of undefined desires ?

" Say, are you happy in the golden march
Of sunlight all across the day ?
Or do you watch the uncertain way
That leads the withering moon on cloudy stairs
Over the heaven's wide arch ?

" Is it towards sorrow or towards joy you lift
The sharpness of your trembling spears ?
Or do you seek, through the grey tears
That blur the sky, in the heart of the triumphing blue,
A deeper, calmer rift ? "

So ; I have tuned my music to the trees,
And there were voices, dim below
Their shrillness, voices swelling slow
In the blue murmur of hills, and a golden cry
And then vast silences.

Aldous Huxley.

54. OAK AND OLIVE

I

THOUGH I was born a Londoner,
    And bred in Gloucestershire,
I walked in Hellas years ago
    With friends in white attire :
And I remember how my soul
    Drank wine as pure as fire.

And when I stand by Charing Cross
    I can forget to hear
The crash of all those smoking wheels,
    When those cold flutes and clear
Pipe with such fury down the street,
    My hands grow moist with fear.

And there's a hall in Bloomsbury
    No more I dare to tread,
For all the stone men shout at me
    And swear they are not dead ;
And once I touched a broken girl
    And knew that marble bled.

II

But when I walk in Athens town
   That swims in dust and sun,
Perverse, I think of London then,
   Where massive work is done,
And with what sweep at Westminster
   The rayless waters run.

I ponder how from Attic seed
   There grew an English tree,
How Byron like his heroes fell,
   Fighting a country free,
And Swinburne took from Shelley's lips
   The kiss of Poetry.

And while our poets chanted Pan
   Back to his pipes and power,
Great Verrall, bending at his desk,
   And searching hour on hour
Found out old gardens, where the wise
   May pluck a Spartan flower.

III

When I go down the Gloucester lanes
   My friends are deaf and blind :
Fast as they turn their foolish eyes
   The Maenads leap behind,
And when I hear the fire-winged feet,
   They only hear the wind.

Have I not chased the fluting Pan
   Through Cranham's sober trees ?
Have I not sat on Painswick Hill
   With a nymph upon my knees,
And she as rosy as the dawn,
   And naked as the breeze ?

IV

But when I lie in Grecian fields,
   Smothered in asphodel,
Or climb the blue and barren hills,
   Or sing in woods that smell
With such hot spices of the South
   As mariners might sell—

Then my heart turns where no sun burns,
   To lands of glittering rain,
To fields beneath low-clouded skies
   New-widowed of their grain,
And Autumn leaves like blood and gold
   That strew a Gloucester lane.

V

Oh, well I know sweet Hellas now,
   And well I knew it then,
When I with starry lads walked out—
   But ah, for home again !
Was I not bred in Gloucestershire,
   One of the Englishmen !

J. E. Flecker.

55. NEW YEAR'S EVE, 1913

OH, Cartmel bells ring soft to-night,
 And Cartmel bells ring clear,
But I lie far away to-night,
 Listening with my dear ;

Listening in a frosty land
 Where all the bells are still
And the small-windowed bell-towers stand
 Dark under heath and hill.

I thought that, with each dying year,
 As long as life should last,
The bells of Cartmel I should hear
 Ring out an aged past :

The plunging, mingling sounds increase
 Darkness's depth and height,
The hollow valley gains more peace
 And ancientness to-night :

The loveliness, the fruitfulness,
 The power of life lived there
Return, revive, more closely press
 Upon that midnight air.

But many deaths have place in men
 Before they come to die ;
Joys must be used and spent, and then
 Abandoned and passed by.

P.T.D. 2—3*

Earth is not ours ; no cherished space
   Can hold us from life's flow,
That bears us thither and thence by ways
   We knew not we should go.

Oh, Cartmel bells ring loud, ring clear,
   Through midnight deep and hoar,
A year new-born, and I shall hear
   The Cartmel bells no more.

                     Gordon Bottomley.

56. BY AVON STREAM

THE jonquils bloom round Samarcand.—
   Maybe ; but lulled by Avon stream,
By hawthorn-scented breezes fanned,
   'Twere mere perversity to dream
      Of Samarcand.

A very heaven the Javan isle !—
   Fond fancy, whither wilt thou stray ?
While bluest skies benignant smile
   On Avon meads, why prate to-day
      Of Javan isle ?

The bulbul 'plains by Omar's shrine.—
   But still I hold, and ever must,
Lark's *tirra-lirra* more divine ;
   And Stratford Church guards dearer dust
      Than Omar's shrine.

                    Arthur Henry Bullen.

57. MARLBOROUGH

I

CROUCHED where the open upland billows down
    Into the valley where the river flows,
She is as any other country town,
    That little lives or marks or hears or knows.

And she can teach but little. She has not
    The wonder and the surging and the roar
Of striving cities. Only things forgot
    That once were beautiful, but now no more,

Has she to give us. Yet to one or two
    She first brought knowledge, and it was for her
To open first our eyes, until we knew
    How great, immeasurably great, we were.

I, who have walked along her downs in dreams,
    And known her tenderness and felt her might,
And sometimes by her meadows and her streams
    Have drunk deep-storied secrets of delight,

Have had my moments there, when I have been
    Unwittingly aware of something more,
Some beautiful aspect that I had seen
    With mute unspeculative eyes before ;

Have had my times, when, though the earth did wear
    Her self-same trees and grasses, I could see
The revelation that is always there,
    But somehow is not always clear to me.

II

So, long ago, one halted on his way
　　And sent his company and cattle on ;
His caravans trooped darkling far away
　　Into the night, and he was left alone.

And he was left alone.　And, lo, a man
　　There wrestled with him till the break of day,
The brook was silent and the night was wan.
　　And when the dawn was come, he passed away.

The sinew of the hollow of his thigh
　　Was shrunken, as he wrestled there alone.
The brook was silent but the dawn was nigh.
　　The stranger named him Israel and was gone.

And the sun rose on Jacob ;　and he knew
　　That he was no more Jacob, but had grown
A more immortal vaster spirit, who
　　Had seen God face to face, and still lived on.

The plain that seemed to stretch away to God,
　　The brook that saw and heard and knew no fear,
Were now the self-same soul as he who stood
　　And waited for his brother to draw near.

For God had wrestled with him, and was gone.
　　He looked around, and only God remained.
The dawn, the desert, he and God were one.
　　—And Esau came to meet him, travel-stained.

III

So, there, when sunset made the downs look new
 And earth gave up her colours to the sky,
And far away the little city grew
 Half into sight, new-visioned was my eye.

I, who have lived, and trod her lovely earth,
 Raced with her winds and listened to her birds,
Have cared but little for their worldly worth,
 Nor sought to put my passion into words.

But now it's different ; and I have no rest
 Because my hand must search, dissect and spell
The beauty that is better not expressed,
 The thing that all can feel, but none can tell.

Charles Hamilton Sorley.

58. THE BALLIOL ROOKS, 1885

THE winter is dead, and the spring is a-dying,
 And summer is marching o'er mountain and
  plain,
And tossing and tumbling and calling and crying
 The Balliol rooks are above us again ;
And watching them wheel on unwearied wings,
I question them softly of vanished things.

 Caw, caw, says every rook,
 To the dreamer his dream, to the scholar his book
 Caw, caw, but the things for me
 Are the windy sky and the windy tree !

O rooks, have you leant from your heights and
    harkened
    From year to year to the whirl below ?
While the suns have flamed and the days have
    darkened,
    Have you marked men ceaselessly come and go,
Loiter a little while here and pass
As the ripple on water, the shadow on grass ?

    Caw, caw, says every rook,
    To the dreamer his dream, to the scholar his book.
    Caw, caw, but the things for me
    Are the windy sky and the windy tree !

The monk with his orisons heavenward rolling,
    The friar of black, and the friar of grey ;
The schoolman stern, and the cavalier trolling
    In court and in cloister his roundelay,
The singer sweet and the preacher pale—
O rooks, can you tell me their wondrous tale ?

    Caw, caw, says every rook,
    To the dreamer his dream, to the scholar his book.
    Caw, caw, but the things for me
    Are the windy sky and the windy tree !

And we that are heirs to their paths and places,
    To the alleys dim and the sunlit towers,
With our hearts on fire, and our eager faces,
    Still hasting along with the hasting hours ;

O rooks, I pray you, come, tell me true :
Was it better the old ? is it better the new ?

Caw, caw, says every rook,
To the dreamer his dream, to the scholar his book.
Caw, caw, but the things for me
Are the windy sky and the windy tree !

And they that shall follow upon us hereafter,
  The men unknown of the unborn years ;
Will they move you at all with their grief and laughter,
  Will you reck, O rooks, of their hopes and fears ;
Or will you but circle scornfully,
And mock at them as you mock at me ?

Caw, caw, says every rook,
To the dreamer his dream, to the scholar his book.
Caw, caw, but the things for me
Are the windy sky and the windy tree !

Frederick S. Boas.

59. AT GRAFTON

GOD laughed when He made Grafton
    That's under Bredon Hill,
A jewel in a jewelled plain.
The seasons work their will
On golden thatch and crumbling stone,
And every soft-lipped breeze
Makes music for the Grafton men
In comfortable trees.

God's beauty over Grafton
Stole into roof and wall,
And hallowed every pavèd path
And every lowly stall,
And to a woven wonder
Conspired with one accord
The labour of the servant,
The labour of the Lord.

And momently to Grafton
Comes in from vale and wold
The sound of sheep unshepherded,
The sound of sheep in fold,
And, blown along the bases
Of lands that set their wide
Frank brows to God, comes chanting
The breath of Bristol tide.

John Drinkwater.

60. OLTON POOLS

Now June walks on the waters,
    And the cuckoo's last enchantment
Passes from Olton pools.

Now dawn comes to my window
Breathing midsummer roses,
And scythes are wet with dew.

Is it not strange for ever
That, bowered in this wonder,
Man keeps a jealous heart ? . . .

That June and the June waters
And birds and dawn-lit roses,
Are gospels in the wind,

Fading upon the deserts,
Poor pilgrim revelations ? . . .
Hist . . . over Olton pools !
John Drinkwater.

61. THE ALDE

How near I walked to Love,
   How long, I cannot tell.
I was like the Alde that flows
Quietly through green level lands,
So quietly, it knows
Their shape, their greenness and their shadows well ;
And then undreamingly for miles it goes
And silently, beside the sea.

Seamews circle over,
The winter wildfowl wings,
Long and green the grasses wave
Between the river and the sea.
The sea's cry, wild or grave,
From bank to low bank of the river rings ;
But the uncertain river, though it crave
The sea, knows not the sea.

Was that indeed salt wind ?
Came that noise from falling
Wild waters on a stony shore ?
Oh, what is this new troubling tide
Of eager waves that pour
Around and over, leaping, parting, recalling ? . . .
How near I moved (as day to same day wore)
And silently, beside the sea !

John Freeman.

62. THE LITTLE WAVES OF BREFFNY

THE grand road from the mountain goes shining to
    the sea,
  And there is traffic on it and many a horse and cart,
But the little roads of Cloonagh are dearer far to me,
  And the little roads of Cloonagh go rambling through
    my heart.

A great storm from the ocean goes shouting o'er the
    hill,
  And there is glory in it and terror on the wind,
But the haunted air of twilight is very strange and still,
  And the little winds of twilight are dearer to my
    mind.

The great waves of the Atlantic sweep storming on
    their way,
  Shining green and silver with the hidden herring
    shoal,

But the Little Waves of Breffny have drenched my
    heart in spray,
  And the Little Waves of Breffny go stumbling
    through my soul.

Eva Gore-Booth.

63. CARROWMORE

IT'S a lonely road through bogland to the lake at
    Carrowmore,
And a sleeper there lies dreaming where the water laps
    the shore ;
Though the moth-wings of the twilight in their purples
    are unfurled,
Yet his sleep is filled with music by the masters of the
    world.

There's a hand is white as silver that is fondling with
    his hair :
There are glimmering feet of sunshine that are dancing
    by him there :
And half-open lips of faery that were dyed a faery red
In their revels where the Hazel Tree its holy clusters
    shed.

" Come away," the red lips whisper, " all the world is
    weary now ;
'Tis the twilight of the ages and it's time to quit the
    plough.
Oh, the very sunlight's weary ere it lightens up the
    dew,
And its gold is changed and faded before it falls to you.

" Though your colleen's heart be tender, a tenderer
      heart is near.
What's the starlight in her glances when the stars are
      shining clear ?
Who would kiss the fading shadow when the flower
      face glows above ?
'Tis the beauty of all Beauty that is calling for your
      love."

Oh, the great gates of the mountain have opened once
      again,
And the sound of song and dancing falls upon the ears
      of men,
And the Land of Youth lies gleaming, flushed with
      rainbow light and mirth,
And the old enchantment lingers in the honey-heart
      of earth.

                                        A. E.

64. CORRYMEELA

O
VER here in England I'm helpin' wi' the hay,
      An' I wisht I was in Ireland the livelong day ;
Weary on the English hay, an' sorra take the wheat !
Och ! Corrymeela an' the blue sky over it.

There' a deep dumb river flowin' by beyont the heavy
      trees,
      This livin' air is moithered wi' the bummin' o' the
      bees ;
I wisht I'd hear the Claddagh burn go runnin' through
      the heat
Past Corrymeela, wi' the blue sky over it.

The people that's in England is richer nor the Jews,
　　There' not the smallest young gossoon but thravels
　　in his shoes !
I'd give the pipe between me teeth to see a barefut
　　child,
　　Och ! Corrymeela an' the low south wind.

Here's hands so full o' money an' hearts so full o' care,
　　By the luck o' love ! I'd still go light for all I did
　　go bare.
" God save ye, *colleen dhas*," I said : the girl she
　　thought me wild.
　　Far Corrymeela, an' the low south wind.

D'ye mind me now, the song at night is mortial hard
　　to raise,
　　The girls are heavy goin' here, the boys are ill to
　　plase ;
When one'st I'm out this workin' hive, 'tis I'll be back
　　again—
　　Ay, Corrymeela, in the same soft rain.

The puff o' smoke from one ould roof before an'
　　English town !
　　For a *shaugh* wid Andy Feelan here I'd give a silver
　　crown,
For a curl o' hair like Mollie's ye'll ask the like in vain,
　　Sweet Corrymeela, an' the same soft rain.
　　　　　　　　　　　　　　　Moira O'Neill.

65. MERRION SQUARE

GREY clouds on the tinted sky,
  A drifting moon, a quiet breeze
Drooping mournfully to cry
In the branches of the trees.

The crying wind, the sighing trees,
  The ruffled stars, the darkness falling
Down the sky, and on the breeze
  A belated linnet calling.

James Stephens.

66. SONG OF THE LARKS AT DAWN

SHEPHERDS who pastures seek
  At dawn may see
From Falterona's peak
  Above Camaldoli
Gleam, beyond forests and wildernesses bleak,
  Both shores of Italy.
Fallen apart are the terrible clouds of the morning
  And men lift up their eyes.

Heaven's troubled continents
  Are rifted, torn :
Thunders, in their forest tents,
  Still seethe and sullenly mourn
When aloft, from the gulfs and the sheer ascents,
  Is a music born.
Hark to that music, laggard mists of the morning,
  And men, lift up your eyes !

For scarce can eye see light
  When the ear's aware
That virginals exquisite
  Are raining from the air—
With sun and pale moon mingling their delight—
  Adorations everywhere !
Now listen and yield the vanquish'd stars of the
    morning
  And men lift up their eyes.

Eddy of golden dust—
  Halo of rays—
Thrilling up, up, as they must
  Die of the life they praise—
The larks, the larks ! that to the earth entrust
  Only their sleeping-place.
From rugged wolds and rock-bound valleys of morning
  The larks like mist arise.

Earth sends them up from hills,
  Her wishes small,
Her cloud of griefs, her wills
  To burst from her own thrall,
And to burn away what chains the soul or chills
  In the God and fount of all.
Open your gates, O ye cities faint for morning,
  And men, lift up your eyes !

Open ! Night's blue Pantheon,
  Thy dark roof-ring
For that escaping pæan
  Of tremblers on the wing

At the unknown threshold of the empyrean
    In myriads soft to sing.
Give way before them, temple-veils of the morning,
    And men, lift up your eyes !

They ascend, ere the red beam
    On heaven grows strong,
Into that amazing stream
    Of Dawn—and float along
In the future, for the future is their dream
    Who roof the world with song.
Open your flowers, O ye mountains spread for morning,
    And men, lift up your eyes !

Hark ! it grows less and less—
    But nothing mars
That rapture beyond guess—
    Beyond our senses' bars—
They drink the virgin Light, the measureless,
    And in it fade, like stars.
They have gone past, the dew-like spirits of morning,
    Beyond the uplifted eyes.

Between two lamps suspended,
    Of Life and Death,
Sun-marshalled and moon-tended
    Man's swift soul journeyeth
To be borne out of the life it hath transcended
    Still, still on a breath ! . . .
To-day we too are the wingèd sons of the morning,
    To-day we will arise !

                    Herbert Trench.

67. THE DARKLING THRUSH

I LEANT upon a coppice gate
    When Frost was spectre-gray,
And Winter's dregs made desolate
    The weakening eye of day.
The tangled bine-stems scored the sky
    Like strings from broken lyres,
And all mankind that haunted nigh
    Had sought their household fires.

The land's sharp features seemed to be
    The Century's corpse outleant,
His crypt the cloudy canopy,
    The wind his death-lament.
The ancient pulse of germ and birth
    Was shrunken hard and dry,
And every spirit upon earth
    Seemed fervourless as I.

At once a voice burst forth among
    The bleak twigs overhead
In a full-hearted evensong
    Of joy illimited ;
An aged thrush, frail, gaunt, and small,
    In blast-beruffled plume,
Had chosen thus to fling his soul
    Upon the growing gloom.

So little cause for carollings
    Of such ecstatic sound
Was written on terrestrial things
    Afar or nigh around,

That I could think there trembled through
    His happy good-night air
Some blessed Hope, whereof he knew
    And I was unaware.

                              Thomas Hardy.

68. BLACKBIRD

HE comes on chosen evenings,
    My blackbird bountiful, and sings
Over the gardens of the town
Just at the hour the sun goes down.
His flight across the chimneys thick,
By some divine arithmetic,
Comes to his customary stack,
And couches there his plumage black,
And there he lifts his yellow bill,
Kindled against the sunset, till
These suburbs are like Dymock woods
Where music has her solitudes,
And while he mocks the winter's wrong
Rapt on his pinnacle of song,
Figured above our garden plots
Those are celestial chimney-pots.

                              John Drinkwater.

69. THE BELLS OF HEAVEN

'TWOULD ring the bells of Heaven
    The wildest peal for years,
If Parson lost his senses
And people came to theirs,

And he and they together
Knelt down with angry prayers
For tamed and shabby tigers,
And dancing dogs and bears,
And wretched, blind pit-ponies,
And little hunted hares.

Ralph Hodgson.

70. THE SNARE

I HEAR a sudden cry of pain !
    There is a rabbit in a snare :
Now I hear the cry again,
    But I cannot tell from where.

But 1 cannot tell from where
    He is calling out for aid ;
Crying on the frightened air,
    Making everything afraid.

Making everything afraid,
    Wrinkling up his little face,
As he cries again for aid ;
    And I cannot find the place !

And I cannot find the place
    Where his paw is in the snare :
Little one ! Oh, little one !
    I am searching everywhere.

James Stephens.

71. THE DONKEY

WHEN fishes flew and forests walked
    And figs grew upon thorn,
Some moment when the moon was blood
    Then surely I was born ;

With monstrous head and sickening cry
    And ears like errant wings,
The devil's walking parody
    On all four-footed things.

The tattered outlaw of the earth,
    Of ancient crooked will ;
Starve, scourge, deride me : I am dumb,
    I keep my secret still.

Fools ! For I also had my hour ;
    One far fierce hour and sweet :
There was a shout about my ears,
    And palms before my feet.

Gilbert Keith Chesterton.

72. MILK FOR THE CAT

WHEN the tea is brought at five o'clock,
    And all the neat curtains are drawn with care,
The little black cat with bright green eyes
Is suddenly purring there.

At first she pretends, having nothing to do,
She has come in merely to blink by the grate,
But, though tea may be late or the milk may be sour,
She is never late.

And presently her agate eyes
Take a soft large milky haze,
And her independent casual glance
Becomes a stiff hard gaze.

Then she stamps her claws or lifts her ears,
Or twists her tail and begins to stir,
Till suddenly all her lithe body becomes
One breathing trembling purr.

The children eat and wriggle and laugh ;
The two old ladies stroke their silk :
But the cat is grown small and thin with desire,
Transformed to a creeping lust for milk.

The white saucer like some full moon descends
At last from the clouds of the table above ;
She sighs and dreams and thrills and glows,
Transfigured with love.

She nestles over the shining rim,
Buries her chin in the creamy sea ;
Her tail hangs loose ; each drowsy paw
Is doubled under each bending knee.

A long dim ecstasy holds her life ;
Her world is an infinite shapeless white,
Till her tongue has curled the last holy drop,
Then she sinks back into the night,

Draws and dips her body to heap
Her sleepy nerves in the great arm-chair,
Lies defeated and buried deep
Three or four hours unconscious there.

Harold Monro.

73. TO A BLACK GREYHOUND

SHINING black in the shining light,
    Inky black in the golden sun,
Graceful as the swallow's flight,
    Light as swallow, wingèd one,
Swift as driven hurricane—
    Double-sinewed stretch and spring,
Muffled thud of flying feet,
    See the black dog galloping,
    Hear his wild foot-beat.

See him lie when the day is dead,
    Black curves curled on the boarded floor.
Sleepy eyes, my sleepy-head—
    Eyes that were aflame before.
Gentle now, they burn no more ;
    Gentle now and softly warm,
With the fire that made them bright
    Hidden—as when after storm
    Softly falls the night.

God of speed, who makes the fire—
    God of Peace, who lulls the same—
God who gives the fierce desire,
    Lust for blood as fierce as flame—

God who stands in Pity's name—
    Many may ye be or less,
Ye who rule the earth and sun :
    Gods of strength and gentleness,
    Ye are ever one.

Julian Grenfell.

74. TIM, AN IRISH TERRIER

IT's wonderful dogs they're breeding now :
    Small as a flea or large as a cow ;
But my old lad Tim he'll never be bet
By any dog that ever he met.
" Come on," says he, " for I'm not kilt yet."

No matter the size of the dog he'll meet,
Tim trails his coat the length o' the street.
D'ye mind his scars an' his ragged ear,
The like of a Dublin Fusilier ?
He's a massacree dog that knows no fear.

But he'd stick to me till his latest breath ;
An' he'd go with me to the gates of death.
He'd wait for a thousand years, maybe,
Scratching the door an' whining for me
If myself were inside in Purgatory.

So I laugh when I hear thim make it plain
That dogs and men never meet again.
For all their talk who'd listen to thim,
With the soul in the shining eyes of him ?
Would God be wasting a dog like Tim ?

W. M. Letts.

75. THE TURKISH TRENCH DOG

NIGHT held me as I crawled and scrambled near
    The Turkish lines.   Above, the mocking stars
Silvered the curving parapet, and clear
Cloud-latticed beams o'erflecked the land with bars ;
I, crouching, lay between
Tense-listening armies, peering through the night,
Twin giants bound by tentacles unseen.
Here in dim-shadowed light
I saw him, as a sudden movement turned
His eyes towards me, glowing eyes that burned
A moment ere his snuffling muzzle found
My trail ; and then as serpents mesmerise
He chained me with those unrelenting eyes,
That muscle-sliding rhythm, knit and bound
In spare-limbed symmetry, those perfect jaws
And soft-approaching pitter-patter paws.
Nearer and nearer like a wolf he crept—
That moment had my swift revolver leapt—
But terror seized me, terror born of shame
Brought flooding revelation.   For he came
As one who offers comradeship deserved,
An open ally of the human race,
And sniffing at my prostrate form unnerved
He licked my face !

Geoffrey Dearmer.

76. SONG FROM CALLIRRHOË

I DANCE and dance !   Another faun,
    A black one, dances on the lawn.
He moves with me, and when I lift
My heels his feet directly shift :

I can't outdance him though I try ;
He dances nimblier than I.
I toss my head, and so does he ;
What tricks he dares to play with me !
I touch the ivy in my hair ;
Ivy he has and finger there.
The spiteful thing to mock me so !
I will outdance him !   Ho, ho, ho !

Michael Field.

77. LULLABY

STRIPPED thee when thou hast and girt
Thy clean night-shirt,
Leap into the soft snug bed ;
Lay down thy head ;
Sleep, and in thy white cot be
A picture for the stars to see.

Cling not to the game that's dead ;
Be glad instead,
After all thy falls and frowns,
That silence drowns
All that any star might see
To make such clear light sad for thee.

Sleep, sleep ;
Down, down,
Through silence good and deep,
Down, down ;

Sink as through a well, each trace
Or of spite, of sulk or frown,
Dying out from thy still face
Till asleep thou dreaming lie,—
A sight to charm the moon on high
And hold her longer in the sky.

T. Sturge Moore.

78. EX ORE INFANTIUM

LITTLE Jesus, wast Thou shy
    Once, and just so small as I ?
And what did it feel like to be
Out of Heaven, and just like me ?
Didst Thou sometimes think of *there*,
And ask where all the angels were ?
I should think that I would cry
For my house all made of sky ;
I would look about the air,
And wonder where my angels were ;
And at waking 'twould distress me—
Not an angel there to dress me !

Hadst Thou ever any toys,
Like us little girls and boys ?
And didst Thou play in Heaven with all
The angels, that were not too tall,
With stars for marbles ?   Did the things
Play *Can you see me ?* through their wings ?

Didst Thou kneel at night to pray,
And didst Thou join Thy hands, this way ?
And did they tire sometimes, being young,
And make the prayer seem very long ?
And dost Thou like it best, that we
Should join our hands to pray to Thee ?
I used to think, before I knew,
The prayer not said unless we do.
And did Thy Mother at the night
Kiss Thee, and fold the clothes in right ?
And didst Thou feel quite good in bed,
Kissed, and sweet, and Thy prayers said ?

Thou canst not have forgotten all
That it feels like to be small :
And Thou know'st I cannot pray
To Thee in my father's way—
When Thou wast so little, say,
Couldst Thou talk Thy Father's way ?—
So, a little Child, come down
And hear a child's tongue like Thy own ;
Take me by the hand and walk,
And listen to my baby-talk.
To Thy Father show my prayer
(He will look, Thou art so fair),
And say : " O Father, I, Thy Son,
Bring the prayer of a little one."

And He will smile, that children's tongue
Has not changed since Thou wast young !
                              Francis Thompson.

79. SHAKESPEARE

IF many a daring spirit must discover
　　The chartless world, why should they glory lack?
Because athwart the skyline they sank over
Few, few, the shipmen be that have come back.

Yet one, wrecked oft, hath by a giddy cord
The rugged head of Destiny regain'd—
One from the maelstrom's lap hath swum aboard—
One from the polar sleep himself unchain'd.

And he, acquainted well with every tone
Of madness whining in his shroudage slender,
From storm and mutiny emerged alone
Self-righted from the dreadful self-surrender :

Rich from the isles where sojourn long is death,
Won back to cool Thames and Elizabeth,
Sea-weary, yes, but human still, and whole,—
A circumnavigator of the soul.

Herbert Trench.

80. I LIKE TO THINK OF SHAKESPEARE

I LIKE to think of Shakespeare, not as when
　　In our old London of the spacious time
He took all amorous hearts with honeyed rhyme ;
Or flung his jest at Burbage and at Ben ;
Or speared the flying follies with his pen ;
Or, in deep hour, made Juliet's love sublime ;
Or from Lear's kindness and Iago's crime
Caught tragic hint of heaven's dark way with men.

These were great memories, but he laid them down.
And when, with brow composed and friendly tread,
He sought the little streets of Stratford town,
That knew his dreams and soon must hold him dead,
I like to think how Shakespeare pruned his rose,
And ate his pippin in his orchard close.

E. K. Chambers.

81. FRIENDS BEYOND

WILLIAM DEWY, Tranter Reuben, Farmer Led-
low late at plough,
    Robert's kin, and John's and Ned's,
And the Squire, and Lady Susan, lie in Mellstock
churchyard now !

" Gone," I call them, gone for good, that group of
local hearts and heads ;
    Yet at mothy curfew-tide,
And at midnight when the noon-heat breathes it back
from walls and leads,

They've a way of whispering to me—fellow-wight
who yet abide—
    In the muted, measured note
Of a ripple under archways, or a lone cave's
stillicide :

" We have triumphed : this achievement turns the
bane to antidote,
    Unsuccesses to success,
Many thought-worn eves and morrows to a morrow
free of thought.

" No more need we corn and clothing, feel of old ter-
    restrial stress ;
        Chill detraction stirs no sigh ;
Fear of death has even bygone us : death gave all
    that we possess."

W. D. : " Ye mid burn the old bass-viol that I set
    such value by."
Squire :   " You may hold the manse in fee,
    You may wed my spouse, may let my children's
    memory of me die."

Lady : " You may have my rich brocades, my laces ;
    take each household key ;
    Ransack coffer, desk, bureau ;
    Quiz the few poor treasures hid there, con the
    letters kept by me."

Far. : " Ye mid zell my favourite heifer, ye mid let
    the charlock grow,
    Foul the grinterns, give up thrift."
Wife : " If ye break my best blue china, children, I
    shan't care or ho."

All :   " We've no wish to hear the tidings how the
    people's fortunes shift ;
    What your daily doings are ;
    Who are wedded, born, divided ; if your lives
    beat slow or swift.

" Curious not the least are we if our intents you
  make or mar,
          If you quire to our old tune,
If the City stage still passes, if the weirs still roar
  afar."

Thus, with very gods' composure, freed those crosses
  late and soon
          Which, in life, the Trine allow
(Why, none witteth), and ignoring all that naps
  beneath the moon,

William Dewy, Tranter Reuben, Farmer Lediow late
  at plough,
          Robert's kin, and John's and Ned's,
And the Squire, and Lady Susan, murmur mildly
  to me now.

                                    Thomas Hardy.

82. THE FIDDLER OF DOONEY

WHEN I play on my fiddle in Dooney,
      Folk dance like a wave of the sea ;
My cousin is priest in Kilvarnet,
My brother in Moharabuiee.

I passed my brother and cousin :
They read in their books of prayer ;
I read in my book of songs
I bought at the Sligo fair.

When we come at the end of time,
To Peter sitting in state,
He will smile on the three old spirits,
But call me first through the gate ;

For the good are always the merry,
Save by an evil chance,
And the merry love the fiddle,
And the merry love to dance :

And when the folk there spy me,
They will all come up to me,
With " Here is the fiddler of Dooney ! "
And dance like a wave of the sea.

William Butler Yeats.

83. THE PLOUGHER

SUNSET and silence ; a man ; around him earth
    savage, earth broken :
Beside him two horses, a plough !

Earth savage, earth broken, the brutes, the dawn-man
    there in the sunset !
And the plough that is twin to the sword, that is
    founder of cities !

" Brute-tamer, plough-maker, earth-breaker, canst
    hear ?   There are ages between us !
Is it praying you are as you stand there, alone in the
    sunset ?

" Surely our sky-born gods can be nought to you,
  Earth-child and Earth-master !
Surely your thoughts are of Pan, or of Wotan or
  Dana !

" Yet why give thought to the gods ? Has Pan led
  your brutes where they stumble ?
Has Wotan put hands to your plough or Dana
  numbed pain of the childbed ?

" What matter your foolish reply, O man, standing
  lone and bowed earthward.
Your task is a day near its close. Give thanks to
  the night-giving God."

Slowly the darkness falls, the broken lands blend with
  the savage,
The brute-tamer stands by the brutes, by a head's
  breadth only above them !

A head's breadth, ay, but therein is Hell's depth and
  the height up to Heaven,
And the thrones of the gods, and their halls and their
  chariots, purples and splendours.

Padraic Colum.

84. THE PENNY WHISTLE

THE new moon hangs like an ivory bugle
  In the naked frosty blue ;
And the ghylls of the forest, already blackened
  By Winter, are blackened anew.

P.T.D. 2—4*

The brooks that cut up and increase the forest,
  As if they had never known
The sun, are roaring with black hollow voices
  Betwixt rage and a moan.

But still the caravan-hut by the hollies
  Like a kingfisher gleams between :
Round the mossed old hearths of the charcoal-burners
  First primroses ask to be seen.

The charcoal-burners are black, but their linen
  Blows white on the line ;
And white the letter the girl is reading
  Under that crescent fine :

And her brother who hides apart in a thicket,
  Slowly and surely playing
On a whistle an olden nursery melody,
  Says far more than I am saying.

                                        Edward Thomas.

85. THE MARKET

A MAN came to me at the fair
    And said, " If you've a poet's tongue,
Tumble up and chant the air
That the stars of morning sung.

" I'll pay you, if you sing it nice,
A penny piece."—I answered flat,
" Sixpence is the proper price
For a ballad such as that."

But he stared and wagged his head,
Growling as he passed along,
" Sixpence ! well, I'll see you dead
Before I pay that for a song."

I saw him buy three pints of stout
With the sixpence—dirty lout !

James Stephens.

86. SEUMAS BEG

A MAN was sitting underneath a tree
   Outside a village, and he asked me what
Name was upon this place, and said that he
Was never here before.   He told a lot
Of stories to me too.   His nose was flat.
I asked him how it happened, and he said
The first mate of the *Mary Anne* done that
With a marling spike one day, but he was dead,
And jolly good job too ; and he'd have gone
A long way to have killed him, and he had
A gold ring in one ear ; the other one
" Was bit off by a crocodile, bedad."
That's what he said.   He taught me how to chew.
He was a real nice man.   He liked me too.

James Stephens.

87. TAM I' THE KIRK

O JEAN, my Jean, when the bell ca's the congrega-
   tion
Owre valley an' hill wi' the ding frae its iron mou',
When a'body's thochts is set on his ain salvation,
    Mine's set on you.

There's a reid rose lies on the Buik o' the Word afore
    ye
That was growin' braw on its bush at the keek o' day,
But the lad that pu'd yon flower i' the mornin's glory,
        He canna pray.

He canna pray ; but there's nane i' the kirk will heed
    him
Whaur he sits sae still his lane at the side o' the wa',
For nane but the reid rose kens what my lassie gie'd
    him—
        It an' us twa !

He canna sing for the sang that his ain he'rt raises,
He canna see for the mist that's afore his een,
And a voice drouns the hale o' the psalms an' the
    paraphrases,
        Cryin' " Jean, Jean, Jean ! "

                            Violet Jacob.

88. THE GOWK

I see the Gowk an' the Gowk sees me
Beside a berry-bush by the apple-tree.
                        Old Scots Rhyme.

TIB, my auntie's a deil to wark,
    Has me risin' afore the sun ;
Aince her heid is abune her sark
    Then the clash o' her tongue's begun !
Warslin', steerin' wi' hens an' swine,
Naucht kens she o' a freend o' mine—
But the Gowk that bides i' the woods o' Dun
        He kens him fine !

Past the yaird an' ahint the stye,
   O the aipples grow bonnilie !
Tib, my auntie, she canna' spy
   Wha comes creepin' to kep wi' me.
Aye ! she'd sort him, for, dod, she's fell !
Whisht now, Jimmie, an' hide yersel'
An' the wise-like bird i' the aipple-tree
      He winna' tell !

Aprile-month, or the aipples flower,
   Tib, my auntie, will rage an' ca' ;
Jimmie lad, she may rin an' glower—
   What care I ?   We'll be far awa' !
Let her seek me the leelang day,
Wha's to tell her the road we'll gae ?
For the cannie Gowk, tho' he kens it a',
      He winna' say !

                              Violet Jacob.

89. THE TWO LAMPLIGHTERS

I NEVER thowt when I grew owd
      I'd tak to leetin' lamps ;
I sud have said, I'd rayther pad
      My hoof on t' road wi' tramps.
But sin I gate that skelp [1] i' t' mine,
      I'm wankle [2] i' my heead ;
So gaffer said, I'd give ower wark
      An' leet town lamps atsteead.

---

[1] Blow.   [2] Unsteady.

At first, when I were liggin' snug
    I' bed, warm as a bee,
'T were hard to rise and get agate
    As sooin as t' clock strake three.
An' I were flaid to hear my steps
    Echoin' on ivery wall ;
An' flaider yet when down by t' church
    Ullets would skreek and call.

But now I'm flaid o' nowt ; I love
    All unkerd [1] sounds o' t' neet,
Frae childer talkin' i' their dreams
    To t' tramp o' p'licemen' feet.
But most of all I love to hark
    To t' song o' t' birds at dawn ;
They wakken up afore it gloams,
    When t' dew ligs thick on t' lawn.

If I feel lonesome, up I look
    To t' sky aboon my heead ;
An' theer's yon stars all glestrin' breet,
    Like daisies in a meead.
But sometimes, when I'm glowerin' up,
    I see the Lord hissen ;
He's doutin' all yon lamps o' Heaven
    That shines on mortal men.

He lowps alang frae star to star,
    As cobby [2] as can be ;
Mebbe He reckons fowk's asleep,
    Wi' niver an eye to see.

[1] Strange, eerie.   [2] Active.

But I hae catched Him at his wark,
    For all He maks no din ;
He leaves a track o' powder'd gowd [1]
    To show where He has bin.

He's got big lamps an' laatle lamps,
    An' lamps that twinkles red ;
I'm capped to see Him dout 'em all
    Afore I'm back i' bed.
But He don't laik about His wark,
    Or stop to hark to t' birds ;
He minds His business, does the Lord,
    An' wastes no gaumless words.

I grow more like Him ivery day,
    For all I walk so lame ;
An', happen, there will coom a time
    I'll beat Him at His game.
Thrang as Throp's wife, I'll dout my lamps
    Afore He's gotten so far ;
An' then I'll shout—" I've won my race,
    I've bet Him by a star."

                F. W. Moorman.

90. A BALLAD-MAKER

ONCE I loved a maiden fair,
    Over the hills and far away,
Lands she had and lovers to spare,
Over the hills and far away.

[1] The Milky Way.

And I was stooped and troubled sore,
And my face was pale, and the coat I wore
Was thin as my supper the night before.
  Over the hills and far away.

Once I passed in the autumn late,
  Over the hills and far away,
Her bawn and byre and painted gate,
  Over the hills and far away.
She was leaning there in the twilight space,
Sweet sorrow was on her fair young face,
And her wistful eyes were away from the place—
  Over the hills and far away.

Maybe she thought as she watched me come,
  Over the hills and far away,
With my awkward stride, and my face so glum,
  Over the hills and far away,
" Spite of his stoop, he still is young ;
They say he goes the Shee among,
Ballads he makes, I've heard them sung
  Over the hills and far away."

She gave me good night in gentle wise,
  Over the hills and far away,
Shyly lifting to mine, dark eyes,
  Over the hills and far away.
What could I do but stop and speak,
And she no longer proud but meek ?
She plucked me a rose like her wild-rose cheek—
  Over the hills and far away.

To-morrow, Mavourneen a sleeveen weds,
  Over the hills and far away,
With corn in haggard and cattle in sheds,
  Over the hills and far away.
And I who have lost her—the dear, the rare—
Well, I got me this ballad to sing at the fair,
'Twill bring enough money to drown my care,
  Over the hills and far away.

                              Padraic Colum.

91. THE PENALTY OF LOVE

IF love should count you worthy, and should deign
    One day to seek your door and be your guest,
  Pause ! ere you draw the bolt and bid him rest,
If in your old content you would remain,
For not alone he enters ; in his train
  Are angels of the mist, the lonely guest
  Dreams of the unfulfilled and unpossessed,
And sorrow, and Life's immemorial pain.

He wakes desires you never may forget,
  He shows you stars you never saw before,
  He makes you share with him, for evermore,
The burden of the world's divine regret.
How wise you were to open not ! and yet,
  How poor if you should turn him from the door !
                          Sidney Royse Lysaght.

92. I WENT INTO THE FIELDS

I WENT into the fields, but you were there
   Waiting for me, so all the summer flowers
Were only glimpses of your starry powers;
Beautiful and inspired dust they were.

I went down by the waters, and a bird
Sang with your voice in all the unknown tones
Of all that self of you I have not heard,
So that my being felt you to the bones.

I went into the house, and shut the door
To be alone, but you were there with me;
All beauty in a little room may be,
Though the roof lean, and muddy be the floor.

Then in my bed I bound my tired eyes
To make a darkness for my weary brain;
But like a presence you were there again,
Being and real, beautiful and wise,

So that I could not sleep, and cried aloud,
"You strange grave thing, what is it you
    would say?"
The redness of your dear lips dimmed to grey,
The waters ebbed, the moon hid in a cloud.

John Masefield.

93. RENOUNCEMENT

I MUST not think of thee ; and, tired yet strong,
　　I shun the love that lurks in all delight—
　The love of thee—and in the blue heaven's height,
And in the dearest passage of a song.
Oh, just beyond the sweetest thoughts that throng
　　This breast, the thought of thee waits hidden yet
　　　bright ;
　　But it must never, never come in sight ;
I must stop short of thee the whole day long.
But when sleep comes to close each difficult day,
　　When night gives pause to the long watch I keep,
And all my bonds I needs must loose apart,
Must doff my will as raiment laid away,—
　　With the first dream that comes with the first sleep,
I run, I run, I am gathered to thy heart.

Alice Meynell.

94. DAWN SHALL OVER LETHE BREAK

LADY, when your lovely head
　　Sinks to lie among the Dead,
And the quiet Places keep
You that so divinely sleep :
Then the Dead shall blessèd be
With a New Solemnity.
For such beauty so descending
Pledges them that death is ending.
Sleep your fill :—But when you wake
Dawn shall over Lethe break.

Hilaire Belloc.

95. LELANT

(In Memory of Thomasine Trenoweth, aged 23)

THE little meadow by the sand,
    Where Tamsin lies, is ringed about
With acres of the scented thyme.
The salt wind blows in all that land ;
The great clouds pace across the skies ;
Rare wanderers from the ferry climb.
One might sleep well enough, no doubt,
    Where Tamsin lies.

Tamsin has sunshine now and wind,
And all in life she might not have,
The silence and the utter peace
That tempest-winnowed spirits find
On slopes that front the western wave.
The white gulls circle without cease
    O'er Tamsin's grave.

E. K. Chambers.

96. THE GREAT LOVER

I HAVE been so great a lover : filled my days
    So proudly with the splendour of Love's praise,
The pain, the calm, and the astonishment,
Desire illimitable, and still content,
And all dear names men use, to cheat despair,
For the perplexed and viewless streams that bear
Our hearts at random down the dark of life.
Now, ere the unthinking silence on that strife

Steals down, I would cheat drowsy Death so far,
My night shall be remembered for a star
That outshone all the suns of all men's days.
Shall I not crown them with immortal praise
Whom I have loved, who have given me, dared with me
High secrets, and in darkness knelt to see
The inenarrable godhead of delight ?
Love is a flame ;—we have beaconed the world's night.
A city :—and we have built it, these and I.
An emperor :—we have taught the world to die.
So, for their sakes I loved, ere I go hence,
And the high cause of Love's magnificence,
And to keep loyalties young, I'll write those names
Golden for ever, eagles, crying flames,
And set them as a banner, that men may know,
To dare the generations, burn, and blow
Out on the wind of Time, shining and streaming . . .

These I have loved :
       White plates and cups, clean-gleaming,
Ringed with blue lines ; and feathery, faery dust ;
Wet roofs, beneath the lamp-light ; the strong crust
Of friendly bread ; and many-tasting food ;
Rainbows ; and the blue bitter smoke of wood ;
And radiant raindrops couching in cool flowers ;
And flowers themselves, that sway through sunny
      hours,
Dreaming of moths that drink them under the moon ;
Then, the cool kindliness of sheets, that soon
Smooth away trouble ; and the rough male kiss
Of blankets ; grainy wood ; live hair that is

Shining and free ; blue-massing clouds ; the keen
Unpassioned beauty of a great machine ;
The benison of hot water ; furs to touch ;
The good smell of old clothes ; and other such—
The comfortable smell of friendly fingers,
Hair's fragrance, and the musty reek that lingers
About dead leaves and last year's ferns . . .

　　　　　　　　　　　　　Dear names,
And thousand other throng to me !   Royal flames ;
Sweet water's dimpling laugh from tap or spring ;
Holes in the ground ; and voices that do sing ;
Voices in laughter, too ; and body's pain,
Soon turned to peace ; and the deep-panting train ;
Firm sands ; the little dulling edge of foam
That browns and dwindles as the wave goes home ;
And washen stones, gay for an hour ; the cold
Graveness of iron ; moist black earthen mould ;
Sleep ; and high places ; footprints in the dew ;
And oaks ; and brown horse-chestnuts, glossy-new ;
And new-peeled sticks ; and shining pools on grass ;—
All these have been my loves. And these shall
　　　pass,
Whatever passes not, in the great hour,
Nor all my passion, all my prayers, have power
To hold them with me through the gate of Death.
They'll play deserter, turn with the traitor breath,
Break the high bond we made, and sell Love's trust
And sacramented covenant to the dust.
—Oh, never a doubt but, somewhere, I shall wake,
And give what's left of love again, and make
New friends, now strangers . . .

But the best I've known,
Stays here, and changes, breaks, grows old, is blown
About the winds of the world, and fades from brains
Of living men, and dies.

               Nothing remains.

O dear my loves, O faithless, once again
This one last gift I give : that after men
Shall know, and later lovers, far-removed,
Praise you, " All these were lovely " ; say, " He
    loved."

                   Rupert Brooke.

97. CLIFTON

I'M here at Clifton, grinding at the mill
   My feet for thrice nine barren years have trod ;
But there are rocks and waves at Scarlett still,
   And gorse runs riot in Glen Chass—thank God !

Alert, I seek exactitude of rule,
   I step, and square my shoulders with the squad ;
But there are blaeberries on old Barrule,
   And Langness has its heather still—thank God !

There is no silence here : the truculent quack
   Insists with acrid shriek my ears to prod,
And, if I stop them, fumes ; but there's no lack
   Of silence still on Carraghyn—thank God !

Pragmatic fibs surround my soul, and bate it
   With measured phrase, that asks the assenting nod ;
I rise, and say the bitter thing, and hate it—
   But Wordsworth's castle's still at Peel—thank God !

O broken life !   O wretched bits of being,
   Unrhythmic, patched, the even and the odd !
But Bradda still has lichens worth the seeing,
   And thunder in her caves—thank God ! thank God !
                        T. E. Brown.

98. A CIDER SONG

To J. S. M.

Extract from a Romance which is not yet written and probably
never will be.

THE wine they drink in Paradise
   They make in Haute Lorraine ;
God brought it burning from the sod
To be a sign and signal rod
That they that drink the blood of God
Shall never thirst again.

The wine they praise in Paradise
They make in Ponterey,
The purple wine of Paradise,
But we have better at the price ;
It's wine they praise in Paradise,
It's cider that they pray.

The wine they want in Paradise
They find in Plodder's End,
The apple wine of Hereford,
Of Hafod Hill and Hereford,
Where woods went down to Hereford,
And there I had a friend.

The soft feet of the blessed go
In the soft western vales,
The road the silent saints accord,
The road from Heaven to Hereford,
Where the apple wood of Hereford
Goes all the way to Wales.

Gilbert Keith Chesterton.

99. FORTUNATUS NIMIUM

I HAVE lain in the sun,
   I have toiled as I might,
I have thought as I would,
And now it is night.

My bed full of sleep,
My heart of content,
For friends that I met
The way that I went.

I welcome fatigue,
While frenzy and care
Like thin summer clouds
Go melting in air.

To dream as I may
And awake when I will
With the song of the birds
And the sun on the hill.

Or death—were it death—
To what should I wake
Who loved in my home
All life for its sake ?

What good have I wrought ?
I laugh to have learned
That joy cannot come
Unless it is earned.

For a happier lot
Than God giveth me
It never hath been
Nor ever shall be.

Robert Bridges.

100. SOLITUDE

WHEN you have tidied all things for the night,
 And while your thoughts are fading to their
  sleep,
You'll pause a moment in the late firelight,
Too sorrowful to weep.

The large and gentle furniture has stood
In sympathetic silence all the day
With that old kindness of domestic wood :
Nevertheless the haunted room will say :
" Some one must be away."

The little dog rolls over half awake,
Stretches his paws, yawns, looking up at you,
Wags his tail very slightly for your sake,
That you may feel he is unhappy too.

A distant engine whistles, or the floor
Creaks, or the wandering night-wind bangs a door.

Silence is scattered like a broken glass.
The minutes prick their ears and run about,
Then one by one subside again and pass
Sedately in, monotonously out.

You bend your head and wipe away a tear
Solitude walks one heavy step more near.
                                    Harold Monro.

101. HEAVY WITH THOUGHT

HEAVY with thought, and burdened with desire,
    O sturdy pilgrim, is it thus you go ?
And is it thus accoutred, is it so,
They start upon the path who dare aspire
To climb the bastion where the peaks of fire,
Home of the thunder burn against the blue ?
And some have reached the goal—but not as you,
Heavy with thought and burdened with desire.

And I, poor cripple, neither faint nor tire ;
My armour is the plumage of the dove,
My thoughts are feathers and my wings are love ;
Higher I soar, and higher yet, and higher,
The dust, the noise, the darkness far above,
Upborne by thought and wingèd with desire.
                                    Cecil Spring-Rice.

102. THE NIGHT

MOST Holy Night, that still dost keep
    Thy keys of all the doors of sleep,
To me when my tired eyelids close
    Give thou repose.

And let the fair lament of them
That chant the day's dead requiem
   Make in my ears, who wakeful lie,
      Sweet Lullaby.

Let them that guard the hornèd Moon
By my bedside their memories croon,
   So shall I have new dreams and blest
      In my brief rest.

Fold thy great wings about my face,
Hide day-dawn from my resting-place,
   And cheat me into false delight,
      Most Holy Night.

Hilaire Belloc.

103. LIGHT

THE night has a thousand eyes,
   And the day but one ;
Yet the light of the bright world dies
   With the dying sun.

The mind has a thousand eyes,
   And the heart but one ;
Yet the light of a whole life dies
   When love is done.

F. W. Bourdillon.

104. SNUG IN MY EASY CHAIR

SNUG in my easy chair,
 I stirred the fire to flame,
Fantastically fair,
The flickering fancies came,
Born of heart's desire :
Amber woodland streaming ;
Topaz islands dreaming ;
Sunset-cities gleaming,
Spire on burning spire ;
Ruddy-windowed taverns ;
Sunshine-spilling wines ;
Crystal-lighted caverns
Of Golconda's mines ;
Summers, unreturning ;
Passion's crater yearning ;
Troy, the ever-burning ;
Shelley's lustral pyre ;
Dragon-eyes, unsleeping ;
Witches' caldrons leaping ;
Golden galleys sweeping
Out from sea-walled Tyre :
Fancies, fugitive and fair,
Flashed with singing through the air ;
Till, dazzled by the drowsy glare,
I shut my eyes to heat and light ;
And saw, in sudden night,
Crouched in the dripping dark,
With steaming shoulders stark,
The man who hews the coal to feed my fire.

Wilfrid Wilson Gibson.

105. MID-MAY, 1918

I

IT shall not me dismay
  That I've grown old and grey ;
Nor tell-tale glass I chide
That will not wrinkles hide :
The visionary gold
That in my heart I hold,
Doth far in worth outshine
All metal from the mine.

II

Of folios I've a store :—
Angelic Henry More,
Lov'd Fuller (wittiest sage)
And Burton's magic page :

There Pliny, Plutarch stand,
Here's Hakewill to my hand,
And thy once far-famed screed,
Apocalyptic Mede.

III

But till the winter eves
Bide there, old printed leaves !
Here's Field o' th' Cloth of Gold
With buttercups untold :

Tall chestnut-candles flare,
Hawthorn makes rich the air,
And tireless cuckoo—hark !—
Calleth from dawn to dark. . . .

Arthur Henry Bullen.

106. IN MERCER STREET

I

A PIPER

A PIPER in the streets to-day
   Set up, and tuned, and started to play,
And away, away, away on the tide
Of his music we started ; on every side
Doors and windows were opened wide,
And men left down their work and came,
And women with petticoats coloured like flame
And little bare feet that were blue with cold,
Went dancing back to the age of gold,
And all the world went gay, went gay,
For half an hour in the street to-day.

II

RAGS AND BONES

Gather 'em, gather 'em, gather 'em O,
He shouts monotonous, jolting slow
His little truck of rags and bones
Over the uneven cobble stones.
Ever about him clink and crowd
The waifs, a many-coloured cloud
All shrilly clamouring, mad with joy,
For sticky sweet, or painted toy.
Hardly a breath is in the air,
Yet every little windmill there
Goes whirling wildly, as though it knew
With every turn what rapture flew

Through all the heavy street, and stirred
The stagnant air, till the sad bird,
High on the wall, takes heart to sing
And hails the simulated Spring.

III

Lark's Song

In Mercer Street the light slants down,
And straightway an enchanted town
Is round him, pinnacle and spire
Flash back, elate, the sudden fire ;
And clear above the silent street
Falls suddenly and strangely sweet
The lark's song.   Bubbling, note on note
Rise fountain-like, o'erflow and float
Tide upon tide, and make more fair
The magic of the sunlit air.
No more the cage can do him wrong,
All is forgotten save his song :
He has forgot the ways of men,
Wide heaven is over him again,
And round him the wide fields of dew
That his first infant mornings knew,
E'er yet the dolorous years had brought
The hours of captive anguish, fraught
With the vile clamour of the street,
The insult of the passing feet,
The torture of the daily round,
The organ's blasphemy of sound.
Sudden some old swift memory brings
The knowledge of forgotten wings,

He springs elate and panting falls
At the rude touch of prison walls.
Silence.   Again the street is grey ;
Shut down the windows.   Work-a-day.
                              Seumas O'Sullivan.

107. THE SHELL

AND then I pressed the shell
          Close to my ear
And listened well,
And straightway like a bell
Came low and clear
The slow, sad murmur of far distant seas,
Whipped by an icy breeze
Upon a shore
Wind-swept and desolate.
It was a sunless strand that never bore
The footprint of a man,
Nor felt the weight
Since time began
Of any human quality or stir
Save what the dreary winds and waves incur.
And in the hush of waters was the sound
Of pebbles rolling round,
For ever rolling with a hollow sound.
And bubbling sea-weeds as the waters go
Swish to and fro
Their long, cold tentacles of shiny grey.
There was no day,
Nor ever came a night
Setting the stars alight

To wonder at the moon :
Was twilight only and the frightened croon,
Smitten to whimpers, of the dreary wind
And waves that journeyed blind—
And then I loosed my ear—O, it was sweet
To hear a cart go jolting down the street.

James Stephens.

108. ROMANCE

Come, come to me !
        I am the Sea,
I am all that can never be ;
The whirling wave, the steady light
Of ships slow sailing out into the night ;
Wind, wave and leaping spray,
And the lands which are very far away ;
Every rainbow-circled shore,
Where you may stay
A night and a day,
No more !
I kiss your eyes and leave them blind ;
I am around you and above ;
I am the road that lies before,
And behind ;
I am Morning—I am Love !
I shake my gleaming
My sun-splashed wings,
Whilst you lie dreaming
Of other things.
The sun shakes your grating
The wind's at the door ;

Oh ! ride forth, for all the world is waiting,
And come back no more !

Am I not fair
With my wishing cap on my gold hair ?
Am I not fleet
Who have feathered shoulders and wingèd feet ?
Listen ! listen ! have you heard
Such a song ever,
As now beneath the wandering moon I sing ?
Each wild-winged bird
Whose throat is mad with Spring
Has sought to learn it and might never !
Listen ! whereso'er I pass
Laughter stirs among the grass,
And the withered tree
Breaks into leaf,
And Grief
Smiles through heavy eyes, tear-laden,
And becomes my waiting-maiden,
Serving me !

I am the sheath, I am the sword,
And I am flame : I set alight
Cities that men may make
Songs of that burning for my sake,
And yield their souls up at a word.
It may be I shall turn my head
And with my eyes' flash strike you dead,
What matters it ?
You will have lived as only they
Who do my bidding may.

Of what avail to sit
In comfort, ease, and slow decay,
Watching the grey ash, bit by bit,
Crumble away ?
What care though I destroy,
Who have re-christened Death and called him Joy,
And have taught Laughter
To the sharp-visaged, horny-fingered Fates.—
Oh ! if I lead you dancing through Hell's gates
What matter what comes after ?

Come, come to me !
I am the moon, I am the sea ;
I am every ship that sails
Trackless waters, knowing not
Where she steers.
I am the light which never fails ;
I am a golden knot
Binding together the loose years.
I sparkle and run
Like ice in the moonlight, like frost in the sun,
And when you have found me, then life has begun.
Therefore be bold,
Of my hand take hold,
And swing in the track of my garment's fold !
Cling to me, follow me, set your heart free ;
I am all that can never be,
A song, a spell, a key of gold,
Which can unlock the earth and the sea :—
Come, come, oh ! come with me !

Lady Margaret Sackville.

109. THE SCHOONER

JUST mark that schooner westward far at sea—
  'Tis but an hour ago
When she was lying hoggish at the quay,
  And men ran to and fro,
And tugged, and stamped, and shoved, and pushed,
  and swore,
And ever and anon, with crapulous glee,
Grinned homage to viragoes on the shore.

So to the jetty gradual she was hauled :
  Then one the tiller took,
And chewed, and spat upon his hand, and bawled ;
  And one the canvas shook
Forth like a mouldy bat ; and one, with nods
And smiles, lay on the bowsprit-end, and called
And cursed the Harbour-master by his gods.

And, rotten from the gunwale to the keel,
  Rat-riddled, bilge-bestank,
Slime-slobbered, horrible, I saw her reel,
  And drag her oozy flank,
And sprawl among the deft young waves, that laughed,
And leapt, and turned in many a sportive wheel,
As she thumped onward with her lumbering draught.

And now, behold ! a shadow of repose
  Upon a line of gray,
She sleeps, that transverse cuts the evening rose—
  She sleeps, and dreams away,
Soft-blended in a unity of rest
All jars, and strifes obscene, and turbulent throes
'Neath the broad benediction of the West—

Sleeps ; and methinks she changes as she sleeps,
    And dies, and is a spirit pure.
Lo ! on her deck an angel pilot keeps
    His lonely watch secure ;
And at the entrance of Heaven's dockyard waits,
Till from Night's leash the fine-breath'd morning leaps,
And that strong hand within unbars the gates.
                    T. E. Brown.

110. A PASSER-BY

WHITHER, O splendid ship, thy white sails crowding,
    Leaning across the bosom of the urgent West,
That fearest nor sea rising, nor sky clouding,
    Whither away, fair rover, and what thy quest ?
    Ah ! soon, when Winter has all our vales opprest.
When skies are cold and misty, and hail is hurling,
    Wilt thou glide on the blue Pacific, or rest
In a summer haven asleep, thy white sails furling.

I there before thee, in the country that well thou
    knowest,
    Already arrived am inhaling the odorous air :
I watch thee enter unerringly where thou goest,
    And anchor queen of the strange shipping there,
    Thy sails for awnings spread, thy masts bare ;
Nor is aught from the foaming reef to the snow-capped
    grandest
    Peak, that is over the feathery palms more fair
Than thou, so upright, so stately, and still thou
    standest.

And yet, O splendid ship, unhailed and nameless,
   I know not if, aiming a fancy, I rightly divine
That thou hast a purpose joyful, a courage blameless,
   Thy port assured in a happier land than mine.
    But for all I have given thee, beauty enough is thine.
As thou, aslant with trim tackle and shrouding,
   From the proud nostril curve of a prow's line
In the offing scatterest foam, thy white sails crowding
                       Robert Bridges.

111. THE OLD SHIPS

I HAVE seen old ships sail like swans asleep
   Beyond the village which men still call Tyre,
With leaden age o'ercargoed, dipping deep
For Famagusta and the hidden sun
That rings black Cyprus with a lake of fire ;
And all those ships were certainly so old—
Who knows how oft with squat and noisy gun,
Questing brown slaves or Syrian oranges,
The pirate Genoese
Hell-raked them till they rolled
Blood, water, fruit and corpses up the hold.
But now through friendly seas they softly run,
Painted the mid-sea blue or shore-sea green,
Still patterned with the vine and grapes in gold.

But I have seen,
Pointing her shapely shadows from the dawn
An image tumbled on a rose-swept bay,
A drowsy ship of some yet older day ;

And, wonder's breath indrawn,
Thought I—who knows—who knows—but in that
    same
(Fished up beyond Aeæa, patched up new
—Stern painted brighter blue—)
That talkative, bald-headed seaman came
(Twelve patient comrades sweating at the oar)
From Troy's doom-crimson shore,
And with great lies about his wooden horse
Set the crew laughing, and forgot his course.
It was so old a ship—who knows, who knows ?
—And yet so beautiful, I watched in vain
To see the mast burst open with a rose,
And the whole deck put on its leaves again.

                     J. E. Flecker.

112. CARGOES

QUINQUIREME of Nineveh from distant Ophir
    Rowing home to haven in sunny Palestine,
With a cargo of ivory,
And apes and peacocks,
Sandalwood, cedarwood, and sweet white wine.

Stately Spanish galleon coming from the Isthmus,
Dipping through the Tropics by the palm-green shores,
With a cargo of diamonds,
Emeralds, amethysts,
Topazes, and cinnamon, and gold moidores.

Dirty British coaster with a salt-caked smoke-stack
Butting through the Channel in the mad March days,
With a cargo of Tyne coal,
Road-rails, pig-lead,
Firewood, iron-ware, and cheap tin trays.

John Masefield.

113. MESSMATES

HE gave us all a good-bye cheerily
    At the first dawn of day ;
We dropped him down the side full drearily
    When the light died away.
It's a dead dark watch that he's a-keeping there,
And a long, long night that lags a-creeping there,
Where the Trades and the tides roll over him
    And the great ships go by.

He's there alone with green seas rocking him
    For a thousand miles round ;
He's there alone with dumb things mocking him,
    And we're homeward bound.
It's a long, lone watch that he's a-keeping there,
And a dead cold night that lags a-creeping there,
While the months and the years roll over him
    And the great ships go by.

I wonder if the tramps come near enough
    As they thrash to and fro,
And the battle-ships' bells ring clear enough
    To be heard down below ;

If through all the lone watch that he's a-keeping there,
And the long, cold night that lags a-creeping there,
The voices of the sailor-men shall comfort him
    When the great ships go by.

Henry Newbolt.

114. SEA FEVER

I MUST go down to the seas again, to the lonely sea
    and the sky,
And all I ask is a tall ship and a star to steer her by ;
And the wheel's kick and the wind's song and the white
    sail's shaking,
And a grey mist on the sea's face, and a grey dawn
    breaking.

I must go down to the seas again, for the call of the
    running tide
Is a wild call and a clear call that may not be denied ;
And all I ask is a windy day with the white clouds
    flying,
And the flung spray and the blown spume, and the
    sea-gulls crying.

I must go down to the seas again, to the vagrant gypsy
    life,
To the gull's way and the whale's way where the wind's
    like a whetted knife ;
And all I ask is a merry yarn from a laughing fellow-
    rover,
And quiet sleep and a sweet dream when the long
    trick's over.

John Masefield.

115. CHORUS FROM HIPPOLYTUS

COULD I take me to some cavern for mine hiding,
   In the hill-tops where the Sun scarce hath trod ;
Or a cloud make the home of mine abiding,
  As a bird among the bird-droves of God !
    Could I wing me to my rest amid the roar
    Of the deep Adriatic on the shore,
Where the water of Eridanus is clear,
  And Phaëthon's sad sisters by his grave
Weep into the river, and each tear
  Gleams, a drop of amber, in the wave !

To the strand of the Daughters of the Sunset,
  The Apple-tree, the singing and the gold ;
Where the mariner must stay him from his onset,
  And the red wave is tranquil as of old ;
    Yea, beyond that Pillar of the End
    That Atlas guardeth, would I wend ;
Where a voice of living waters never ceaseth
  In God's quiet garden by the sea,
And Earth, the ancient life-giver, increaseth
  Joy among the meadows, like a tree.

Gilbert Murray.

116. THE SONG OF THE UNGIRT RUNNERS

WE swing ungirded hips,
   And lightened are our eyes,
The rain is on our lips,
We do not run for prize.

We know not whom we trust
Nor whitherward we fare,
But we run because we must
   Through the great wide air.

The waters of the seas
Are troubled as by storm.
The tempest strips the trees
And does not leave them warm.
Does the tearing tempest pause ?
Do the tree tops ask it why ?
So we run without a cause
   'Neath the big bare sky.

The rain is on our lips,
We do not run for prize.
But the storm the water whips
And the wave howls to the skies.
The winds arise and strike it
And scatter it like sand,
And we run because we like it
   Through the broad bright land.

             Charles Hamilton Sorley.

117. THE CAVES OF AUVERGNE

HE carved the red deer and the bull
   Upon the smooth cave rock,
Returned from war with belly full,
   And scarred with many a knock,
He carved the red deer and the bull
   Upon the smooth cave rock.

The stars flew by the cave's wide door,
    The clouds wild trumpets blew,
Trees rose in wild dreams from the floor,
    Flowers with dream faces grew
Up to the sky, and softly hung
    Golden and white and blue.

The woman ground her heap of corn,
    Her heart a guarded fire ;
The wind played in his trembling soul
    Like a hand upon a lyre,
The wind drew faintly on the stone
    Symbols of his desire :

The red deer of the forest dark,
    Whose antlers cut the sky,
That vanishes into the mirk
    And like a dream flits by,
And by an arrow slain at last
    Is but the wind's dark body.

The bull that stands in marshy lakes
    As motionless and still
As a dark rock jutting from a plain
    Without a tree or hill ;
The bull that is the sign of life,
    Its sombre, phallic will.

And from the dead, white eyes of them
    The wind springs up anew,
It blows upon the trembling heart,
    And bull and deer renew
Their flitting life in the dim past
    When that dead Hunter drew.

I sit beside him in the night,
    And, fingering his red stone,
I chase through endless forests dark
    Seeking that thing unknown,
That which is not red deer or bull,
    But which by them was shown :

By those stiff shapes in which he drew
    His soul's exalted cry,
When flying down the forest dark
    He slew and knew not why,
When he was filled with song, and strength
    Flowed to him from the sky.

The wind blows from red deer and bull,
    The clouds wild trumpets blare,
Trees rise in wild dreams from the earth,
    Flowers with dream-faces stare,
O Hunter, your own shadow stands
    Within your forest lair !

                  Walter J. Turner.

118. ECSTASY

I SAW a frieze on whitest marble drawn
    Of boys who sought for shells along the shore,
Their white feet shedding pallor in the sea,
The shallow sea, the spring-time sea of green
That faintly creamed against the cold, smooth pebbles.

The air was thin, their limbs were delicate,
The wind had graven their small eager hands
To feel the forests and the dark nights of Asia
Behind the purple bloom of the horizon,
Where sails would float and slowly melt away.

Their naked, pure, and grave unbroken silence
Filled the soft air as gleaming, limpid water
Fills a spring sky those days when rain is lying
In shattered bright pools on the wind-dried roads,
And their sweet bodies were wind-purified.

One held a shell unto his shell-like ear
And there was music carven in his face,
His eyes half-closed, his lips just breaking open
To catch the lulling, mazy, coralline roar
Of numberless caverns filled with singing seas.

And all of them were hearkening as to singing
Of far-off voices thin and delicate,
Voices too fine for any mortal wind
To blow into the whorls of mortal ears—
And yet those sounds flowed from their grave, sweet
    faces.

And as I looked I heard that delicate music,
And I became as grave, as calm, as still
As those carved boys.   I stood upon that shore,
I felt the cool sea dream around my feet,
My eyes were staring at the far horizon;

And the wind came and purified my limbs,
And the stars came and set within my eyes,
And snowy clouds rested upon my shoulders,
And the blue sky shimmered deep within me,
And I sang like a carven pipe of music.

W. J. Turner.

119. THE WAR SONG OF THE SARACENS

WE are they who come faster than fate: we are
they who ride early or late:
We storm at your ivory gate: Pale Kings of the
Sunset, beware !
Not on silk nor in samet we lie, not in curtained
solemnity die
Among women who chatter and cry, and children who
mumble a prayer.
But we sleep by the ropes of the camp, and we rise
with a shout, and we tramp
With the sun or the moon for a lamp, and the spray
of the wind in our hair.

From the lands, where the elephants are, to the forts
of Merou and Balghar,
Our steel we have brought and our star to shine on
the ruins of Rum.
We have marched from the Indus to Spain, and by God
we will go there again ;
We have stood on the shore of the plain where the
Waters of Destiny boom.
A mart of destruction we made at Jalula where men
were afraid,

For death was a difficult trade, and the sword was a
    broker of doom ;

And the Spear was a Desert Physician who cured not
    a few of ambition,
And drave not a few to perdition with medicine bitter
    and strong ;
And the shield was a grief to the fool and as bright
    as a desolate pool,
And as straight as the rock of Stamboul when their
    cavalry thundered along :
For the coward was drowned with the brave when our
    battle sheered up like a wave,
And the dead to the desert we gave, and the glory
    to God in our song.

J. E. Flecker.

120. THE WIFE OF LLEW

A<small>ND</small> Gwydion said to Math, when it was Spring :
    " Come now and let us make a wife for Llew,"
And so they broke broad boughs yet moist with dew,
And in a shadow made a magic ring :
They took the violet and the meadow-sweet
To form her pretty face, and for her feet
They built a mound of daisies on a wing,
And for her voice they made a linnet sing
In the wide poppy blowing for her mouth.
And over all they chanted twenty hours.
And Llew came singing from the azure south
And bore away his wife of birds and flowers.

Francis Ledwidge.

121 THE OXEN

CHRISTMAS Eve, and twelve of the clock.
    " Now they are all on their knees,"
An elder said as we sat in a flock
    By the embers in hearthside ease.

We pictured the meek mild creatures where
    They dwelt in their strawy pen,
Nor did it occur to one of us there
    To doubt they were kneeling then.

So fair a fancy few would weave
    In these years !   Yet, I feel,
If someone said on Christmas Eve,
    " Come ; see the oxen kneel

" In the lonely barton by yonder coomb
    Our childhood used to know,"
I should go with him in the gloom,
    Hoping it might be so.

Thomas Hardy.

122 THE LISTENERS

" Is there anybody there ? " said the Traveller,
    Knocking on the moonlit door ;
And his horse in the silence champed the grasses
    Of the forest's ferny floor :
And a bird flew up out of the turret,
    Above the Traveller's head :
And he smote upon the door again a second time ;
    " Is there anybody there ? " he said.

But no one descended to the Traveller ;
  No head from the leaf-fringed sill
Leaned over and looked into his grey eyes,
  Where he stood perplexed and still.
But only a host of phantom listeners
  That dwelt in the lone house then
Stood listening in the quiet of the moonlight
  To that voice from the world of men :
Stood thronging the faint moonbeams on the dark
    stair,
  That goes down to the empty hall,
Hearkening in an air stirred and shaken
  By the lonely Traveller's call.
And he felt in his heart their strangeness,
  Their stillness answering his cry,
While his horse moved, cropping the dark turf,
  'Neath the starred and leafy sky ;
For he suddenly smote on the door, even
  Louder, and lifted his head :—
" Tell them I came, and no one answered,
  That I kept my word," he said.
Never the least stir made the listeners,
  Though every word he spake
Fell echoing through the shadowiness of the still house
  From the one man left awake :
Ay, they heard his foot upon the stirrup,
  And the sound of iron on stone,
And how the silence surged softly backward,
  When the plunging hoofs were gone.

                    Walter de la Mare.

123. THE CHANGELING

Toll no bell for me, dear Father, dear Mother,
   Waste no sighs ;
There are my sisters, there is my little brother
   Who plays in the place called Paradise,
Your children all, your children for ever ;
         But I, so wild,
Your disgrace, with the queer brown face, was never,
   Never, I know, but half your child !

In the garden at play, all day, last summer,
         Far and away I heard
The sweet " tweet-tweet " of a strange new-comer,
   The dearest, clearest call of a bird.
It lived down there in the deep green hollow,
   My own old home, and the fairies say
The word of a bird is a thing to follow,
   So I was away a night and a day.

One evening, too, by the nursery fire,
   We snuggled close and sat round so still,
When suddenly as the wind blew higher,
   Something scratched on the window-sill.
A pinched brown face peered in—I shivered ;
   No one listened or seemed to see ;
The arms of it waved and the wings of it quivered,
   Whoo—I knew it had come for me ;
   Some are as bad as bad can be !
All night long they danced in the rain,
Round and round in a dripping chain,

Threw their caps at the window-pane,
  Tried to make me scream and shout
  And fling the bedclothes all about :
I meant to stay in bed that night,
And if only you had left a light
  They would never have got me out.

Sometimes I wouldn't speak, you see,
  Or answer when you spoke to me,
Because in the long, still dusks of Spring
You can hear the whole world whispering ;
  The shy green grasses making love,
  The feathers grow on the dear, grey dove,
  The tiny heart of the redstart beat,
  The patter of the squirrel's feet,
The pebbles pushing in the silver streams,
The rushes talking in their dreams,
  The swish-swish of the bat's black wings,
  The wild-wood bluebell's sweet ting-tings,
    Humming and hammering at your ear,
    Everything there is to hear
In the heart of hidden things,
  But not in the midst of the nursery riot,
  That's why I wanted to be quiet,
    Couldn't do my sums, or sing,
    Or settle down to anything.
  And when, for that, I was sent upstairs
  I *did* kneel down to say my prayers ;
But the King who sits on your high church steeple
Has nothing to do with us fairy people !

'Times I pleased you, dear Father, dear Mother,
  Learned all my lessons and liked to play,
And dearly I loved the little pale brother
  Whom some other bird must have called away.
Why did They bring me here to make me
  Not quite bad and not quite good,
Why, unless They're wicked, do They want, in spite, to take me
  Back to their wet, wild wood ?
Now, every night I shall see the windows shining,
  The gold lamp's glow, and the fire's red gleam,
While the best of us are twining twigs and the rest of us are whining
  In the hollow by the stream.
Black and chill are Their nights on the wold ;
  And They live so long and They feel no pain :
I shall grow up, but never grow old,
I shall always, always be very cold,
  I shall never come back again !

Charlotte Mew.

124. A FAERY SONG

WHEN through a thousand eyes
    Heaven is gleaming,
Troop there folk wee and wise,
Laden with dreaming ;
Packs full of finest gold
Culled from the river,
Where sunbeams manifold
Shimmer and shiver ;

Packs full of diamonds they
Gathered at morning,
Down by the meadow-way,
Grasses adorning ;
Packs full of lovesongs more
Sweet than a lover's,
Filched from a troubadour
Feathered pelt covers.
>Come away !
>Come and play
>Life with the faeries,
>Lest you grow old and grey
>Dwelling where care is.

Down from the hillsides green,
Up from the valleys,
Round her Queen Mab, I ween,
All her host rallies ;
For him who wakes to see
—Gladdest of mortals—
Faeryland verily
Opens her portals ;
Every elf on the ground,
Lo, his pack flinging,
See them dance round and round,
Hark to their singing !
>Come away !
>Come and play
>Life with the faeries,
>Lest you grow old and grey
>Dwelling where care is.

Work-a-day !   Work-a-day !
Counting your sorrow ;
Night is the hour of play
Ere dawns the morrow.
Here there be gold and stones,
Love in full measure ;
He who sleeps lightly owns
Princeliest treasure.
Gather then while ye may
Dreams full of gladness,
Though with the turn of day
Care come and sadness.

Come away !
Come and play
Life with the faeries,
Lest you grow old and grey
Dwelling where care is.

Madeleine Nightingale.

125. PISKIES

(Writ in Devon)

THERE'S piskies up to Dartymoor,
    An' tidden gude yew zay there bain't.
I've felt 'em grawpin' at my heart,
I've heard their voices callin' faint,
I've knawed a man be cruel down—
His soul fair stogged an' heavy-like—
Climb up to brawken Zaddle Tor
An' bare his head vor winds to strike.

An' all the gert black mawky griefs,
An' all the pain an' vog an' grime,
Have blawed away and left en clear
Like vuzz-bush vires in swalin' time.
An' what med do so brave a thing
As thic' white spells to tak an' weave,
But li'l piskies' vitty hands,
Or God Himself as give 'em leave ?
But tidden Him would stop an' spy
From Widdicombe to Cranmer Pule,
To maze the schemin' li'l heart
Of every Jacky-Lantern fule !
For mebbe 'tis a lonesome rod
Or heather blooth, or peaty ling,
Or nobbut just a rainy combe—
The spell that meks 'ee tek an' sing.
An' this I knaw, the li'l tods
Be ever callin' silver faint.
There's piskies up to Dartymoor,
An' tidden gude yew zay there bain't.

> *T. P. Cameron Wilson.*

126. THE STOLEN CHILD

WHERE dips the rocky highland
　　Of Sleuth Wood in the lake,
There lies a leafy island
Where flapping herons wake
The drowsy water-rats ;
There we've hid our faery vats,

Full of berries,
And of reddest stolen cherries.
Come away, O human child!
To the waters and the wild
With a faery, hand in hand,
For the world's more full of weeping than you
*   can understand.*

Where the wave of moonlight glosses
The dim gray sands with light,
Far off by furthest Rosses
We foot it all the night,
Weaving olden dances,
Mingling hands and mingling glances
Till the moon has taken flight ;
To and fro we leap
And chase the frothy bubbles,
While the world is full of troubles
And is anxious in its sleep.
Come away, O human child!
To the waters and the wild
With a faery, hand in hand,
For the world's more full of weeping than you
*   can understand.*

Where the wandering water gushes
From the hills above Glen-Car,
In pools among the rushes
That scarce could bathe a star,
We seek for slumbering trout,
And whispering in their ears

Give them unquiet dreams ;
Leaning softly out
From ferns that drop their tears
Over the young streams.
Come away, O human child !
To the waters and the wild
With a faery, hand in hand,
For the world's more full of weeping than you
    can understand.

Away with us he's going,
The solemn-eyed :
He'll hear no more the lowing
Of the calves on the warm hillside ;
Or the kettle on the hob
Sing peace into his breast,
Or see the brown mice bob
Round and round the oatmeal-chest.
For he comes, the human child,
To the waters and the wild
With a faery, hand in hand,
From a world more full of weeping than he
    can understand.

                    William Butler Yeats.

127. THE VOICE

THE wind blows out of the gates of the day
    The wind blows over the lonely of heart
And the lonely of heart is withered away,
While the faeries dance in a place apart,

Shaking their milk-white feet in a ring,
Tossing their milk-white arms in the air ;
For they hear the wind laugh, and murmur and sing
Of a land where even the old are fair,
And even the wise are merry of tongue ;
But I heard a reed of Coolaney say,
" When the wind has laughed and murmured and sung,
The lonely of heart is withered away ! "

William Butler Yeats.

128. THE THREE STRANGERS

Far are those tranquil hills,
    Dyed with fair evening's rose ;
On urgent, secret errand bent,
     A traveller goes.

Approach him strangers three,
Barefooted, cowled ; their eyes
Scan the lone, hastening solitary
    With dumb surmise.

One instant in close speech
With them he doth confer :
God-sped, he hasteneth on,
    That anxious traveller . . .

I was that man—in a dream :
And each world's night in vain
I patient wait on sleep to unveil
    Those vivid hills again.

Would that they three could know
How yet burns on in me
Love—from one lost in Paradise—
For their grave courtesy.

Walter de la Mare.

129. UXBRIDGE ROAD

THE Western Road goes streaming out to seek the
cleanly wild,
It pours the city's dim desires towards the undefiled,
It sweeps betwixt the huddled homes about its eddies
grown
To smear the little space between the city and the
sown :
The torments of that seething tide who is there that
can see ?
There's one who walked with starry feet the western
road by me !

He is the Drover of the soul ; he leads the flock of men
All wistful on that weary track, and brings them back
again.
The dreaming few, the slaving crew, the motley caste
of life—
The wastrel and artificer, the harlot and the wife—
They may not rest, for ever pressed by one they
cannot see :
The one who walked with starry feet the western road
by me.

He drives them east, he drives them west, between the
    dark and light ;
He pastures them in city pens, he leads them home at
    night.
The towery trams, the threaded trains, like shuttles
    to and fro
To weave the web of working days in ceaseless travel
    go.
How harsh the woof, how long the weft ! who shall
    the fabric see ?
The one who walked with starry feet the western road
    by me !

Throughout the living joyful year at lifeless tasks to
    strive,
And scarcely at the end to save gentility alive ;
The villa plot to sow and reap, to act the villa lie,
Beset by villa fears to live, midst villa dreams to die ;
Ah, who can know the dreary woe ? and who the
    splendour see ?
The one who walked with starry feet the western road
    by me.

Behold ! he lent me as we went the vision of the seer ;
Behold ! I saw the life of men, the life of God shine
    clear.
I saw the hidden Spirit's thrust ; I saw the race fulfil
The spiral of its steep ascent, predestined of the Will.
Yet not unled, but shepherded by one they may not
    see—
The one who walked with starry feet the western road
    by me !
                      Evelyn Underhill.

130. IMMANENCE

I COME in the little things,
   Saith the Lord :
Not borne on morning wings
Of majesty, but I have set My Feet
Amidst the delicate and bladed wheat
That springs triumphant in the furrowed sod.
There do I dwell, in weakness and in power ;
Not broken or divided, saith our God !
In your strait garden plot I come to flower :
About your porch My Vine
Meek, fruitful, doth entwine ;
Waits, at the threshold, Love's appointed hour.

I come in the little things,
Saith the Lord :
Yea ! on the glancing wings
Of eager birds, the softly pattering feet
Of furred and gentle beasts, I come to meet
Your hard and wayward heart.   In brown bright eyes
That peep from out the brake, I stand confest.
On every nest
Where feathery Patience is content to brood
And leaves her pleasure for the high emprize
Of motherhood—
There doth My Godhead rest.

I come in the little things,
Saith the Lord :
My starry wings

I do forsake,
Love's highway of humility to take :
Meekly I fit my stature to your need.
In beggar's part
About your gates I shall not cease to plead—
As man, to speak with man—
Till by such art
I shall achieve My Immemorial Plan,
Pass the low lintel of the human heart.
                              Evelyn Underhill.

131. THE BUGLER

GOD dreamed a man ;
      Then, having firmly shut
Life like a precious metal in his fist,
Withdrew, His labour done.   Thus did begin
Our various divinity and sin.
For some to ploughshares did the metal twist,
And others—dreaming empires—straightway cut
Crowns for their aching foreheads.   Others beat
Long nails and heavy hammers for the feet
Of their forgotten Lord.   (Who dare to boast
That he is guiltless ?)   Others coined it : most
Did with it—simply nothing.   (Here, again,
Who cries his innocence ?)   Yet doth remain
Metal unmarred, to each man more or less,
Whereof to fashion perfect loveliness.

For me, I do but bear within my hand
(For sake of Him our Lord, now long forsaken)
A simple bugle such as may awaken

With one high morning note a drowsing man :
That wheresoe'er within my motherland
The sound may come, 'twill echo far and wide
Like pipes of battle calling up a clan,
Trumpeting men through beauty to God's side.

F. W. Harvey.

132. THE TWILIGHT OF EARTH

THE wonder of the world is o'er :
   The magic from the sea is gone :
There is no unimagined shore,
   No islet yet to venture on.
The Sacred Hazels' blooms are shed,
The Nuts of Knowledge harvested.

Oh, what is worth this lore of age
   If time shall never bring us back
Our battle with the gods to wage
   Reeling along the starry track.
The battle rapture here goes by
In warring upon things that die.

Let be the tale of him whose love
   Was sighed between white Deirdre's breasts,
It will not lift the heart above
   The sodden clay on which it rests.
Love once had power the gods to bring
All rapt on its wild wandering.

We shiver in the falling dew,
    And seek a shelter from the storm :
When man these elder brothers knew
    He found the mother nature warm,
A hearth fire blazing through it all,
A home without a circling wall.

We dwindle down beneath the skies,
    And from ourselves we pass away ;
The paradise of memories
    Grows ever fainter day by day.
The shepherd stars have shrunk within,
The world's great night will soon begin.

Will no one, ere it is too late,
    Ere fades the last memorial gleam,
Recall for us our earlier state ?
    For nothing but so vast a dream
That it would scale the steeps of air
Could rouse us from so vast despair.

The power is ours to make or mar
    Our fate as on the earliest morn,
The Darkness and the Radiance are
    Creatures within the spirit born.
Yet, bathed in gloom too long, we might
Forget how we imagined light.

Not yet are fixed the prison bars ;
    The hidden light the spirit owns
If blown to flame would dim the stars
    And they who rule them from their thrones :

And the proud sceptred spirits thence
Would bow to pay us reverence.

Oh, while the glory sinks within
    Let us not wait on earth behind,
But follow where it flies, and win
    The glow again, and we may find
Beyond the Gateways of the Day
Dominion and ancestral sway.

A. E.

133. HOPE IN FAILURE

THOUGH now thou hast failed and art fallen, despair
    not because of defeat,
Though lost for a while be thy heaven and weary of
    earth be thy feet,
For all will be beauty about thee hereafter through
    sorrowful years,
And lovely the dews for thy chilling and ruby thy
    heart-drip of tears.

The eyes that had gazed from afar on a beauty that
    blinded the eyes
Shall call forth its image for ever, its shadow in alien
    skies.
The heart that had striven to beat in the heart of the
    Mighty too soon
Shall still of that beating remember some errant and
    faltering tune.

For thou hast but fallen to gather the last of the secrets
    of power;
The beauty that breathes in thy spirit shall shape of
    thy sorrow a flower,
The pale bud of pity shall open the bloom of its
    tenderest rays,
The heart of whose shining is bright with the light of
    the Ancient of Days.

A. E.

134. THE MYSTERY

HE came and took me by the hand
    Up to a red rose tree,
He kept His meaning to Himself
    But gave a rose to me.
I did not pray Him to lay bare
    The mystery to me,
Enough the rose was Heaven to smell,
    And His own face to see.

Ralph Hodgson.

135. I SEE HIS BLOOD UPON THE ROSE

I SEE His blood upon the rose
    And in the stars the glory of His eyes,
His body gleams amid eternal snows,
His tears fall from the skies.

I see His face in every flower;
The thunder and the singing of the birds
Are but His voice—and carven by His power
Rocks are His written words.

All pathways by His feet are worn,
His strong heart stirs the ever-beating sea,
His crown of thorns is twined with every thorn,
His cross is every tree.

Joseph Mary Plunkett.

136. HE IS THE LONELY GREATNESS

HE is the lonely greatness of the world—
    (His eyes are dim),
His power it is holds up the Cross
    That holds up Him.

He takes the sorrow of the threefold hour—
    (His eyelids close),
Round Him and round, the wind—His Spirit—where
    It listeth blows.

And so the wounded greatness of the World
    In silence lies—
And death is shattered by the light from out
    Those darkened eyes.

Madeleine Caron Rock.

137. THE FINAL MYSTERY

(This myth, of Egyptian origin, formed part of the instruction
given to those initiated in the Orphic mysteries, and written versions
of it were buried with the dead.)

HEAR now, O Soul, the last command of all—
    When thou hast left thine every mortal mark,
And by the road that lies beyond recall
Won through the desert of the Burning Dark,
Thou shalt behold within a garden bright
A well, beside a cypress ivory-white.

Still is that well, and in its waters cool
White, white and windless, sleeps that cypress tree:
Who drinks but once from out her shadowy pool
Shall thirst no more to all eternity.
Forgetting all, by all forgotten clean,
His soul shall be with that which hath not been.

But thou, though thou be trembling with thy dread,
And parched with thy desire more fierce than flame,
Think on the stream wherefrom thy life was fed,
And that diviner fountain whence it came.
Turn thee and cry—behold, it is not far—
Unto the hills where living waters are.

" Lord, though I lived on earth, the child of earth,
Yet was I fathered by the starry sky:
Thou knowest I came not of the shadows' birth,
Let me not die the death that shadows die.
Give me to drink of the sweet spring that leaps
From Memory's fount, wherein no cypress sleeps."

Then shalt thou drink, O Soul, and therewith slake
The immortal longing of thy mortal thirst;
So of thy Father's life shalt thou partake,
And be for ever that thou wert at first.
Lost in remembered loves, yet thou more thou
With them shalt reign in never-ending *Now*.

Henry Newbolt.

138. THE LAUNCH

Forth, to the alien gravity,
    Forth, to the laws of ocean, we
  Builders on earth by laws of land
Entrust this creature of our hand
Upon the calculated sea.

Fast bound to shore we cling, we creep,
And make our ship ready to leap
  Light to the flood, equipped to ride
  The strange conditions of the tide—
New weight, new force, new world : the Deep.

Ah thus—not thus—the Dying, kissed,
Cherished, exhorted, shriven, dismissed ;
  By all the eager means we hold
  We, warm, prepare him for the cold,
To keep the incalculable tryst.

Alice Meynell.

139. EPILOGUE TO "A JUDGEMENT IN HEAVEN"

Virtue may unlock hell, or even
    A sin turn in the wards of Heaven,
(As ethics of the text-book go,)
So little men their own deeds know,
Or through the intricate *mêlée*
Guess whitherward draws the battle-sway ;

So little, if they know the deed,
Discern what therefrom shall succeed.
To wisest moralists 'tis but given
To work rough border-law of Heaven,
Within this narrow life of ours,
These marches 'twixt delimitless Powers.
Is it, if Heaven the future showed,
Is it the all-severest mode
To see ourselves with the eyes of God ?
God rather grant, at His assize,
He see us not with our own eyes !

Heaven, which man's generations draws,
Nor deviates into replicas,
Must of as deep diversity
In judgement as creation be.
There is no expeditious road
To pack and label men for God,
And save them by the barrel-load.
Some may perchance, with strange surprise,
Have blundered into Paradise.
In vasty dusk of life abroad,
They fondly thought to err from God,
Nor knew the circle that they trod ;
And, wandering all the night about,
Found them at morn where they set out.
Death dawned ; Heaven lay in prospect wide :—
Lo ! they were standing by His side !

Francis Thompson.

140. ENVOY

Go, songs, for ended is our brief, sweet play ;
  Go, children of swift joy and tardy sorrow :
And some are sung, and that was yesterday,
  And some unsung, and that may be to-morrow.

Go forth ; and if it be o'er stony way,
  Old joy can lend what newer grief must borrow :
And it was sweet, and that was yesterday,
  And sweet is sweet, though purchasèd with sorrow.

Go, songs, and come not back from your far way :
  And if men ask you why ye smile and sorrow,
Tell them ye grieve, for your hearts know To-day,
  Tell them ye smile, for your eyes know To-morrow
              Francis Thompson.

INDEX OF FIRST LINES